ONE WHO BELIEVED

True Stories of Faith

ONE WHO BELIEVED

True Stories of Faith

Dr. Robert B. Pamplin, Jr.
and Thomas K. Worcester

Christ Community Church
P.O. Box 88
Dundee, Oregon 97115

ONE WHO BELIEVED
True Stories of Faith

Dedication

Dedicated to those honored women and men, living or deceased, who have made this book possible by their exemplary life of faith.

Acknowledgement

Many of the stories included in this volume were extracted from biographies about the subjects. The authors gratefully acknowledge the initial works that provided information for these stories as credited elsewhere in this book.

CONTENTS

CHRIST COMMUNITY CHURCH

Introduction

The objective of Christ Community Church is to maintain the preaching of the whole counsel of God, according to the doctrines of both the Old and New Testaments. The church was established to strengthen Christians in their belief, and to introduce Christian principles to those whose lives are outside the ways of Christ.

In addition to offering individuals an opportunity to share these beliefs through a series of "One Who Believed" radio profiles of prominent Christians, the church operates a food ministry to provide nutritional resources to the needy.

The outreach of Christ Community Church directly reflects the Christian beliefs and social philosophies of its pastor and patron, Dr. Robert B. Pamplin, Jr.: that assistance to fellow man is an investment in the total person, something that can be increased with judicious thought and planning.

Dr. Pamplin is committed to helping some members of the society who are less fortunate than others, but in a creative way which allows individuals to become contributing partners in the society. He believes deeply in giving – and in giving deeply – yet also seeks innovative ways to increase the value of gifts, whether they be time, talent or money.

For example, one of the ministries of Christ

Community Church is to provide ground beef, canned vegetables and fruits, peanut butter and other food items for the poor and children's homes. Relief agencies selected to receive the food are chosen because part of their operation is a counseling program that attempts to regenerate the person to become once again a productive member of society. The program concentrates also on those agencies that have a Christian emphasis in their own social service. The church is especially interested in helping children's homes, as children often tend to be innocent victims of their environment and circumstances.

The phrase "innovative economics" best describes the ways in which the gifts of Christ Community Church are enhanced above their normal value. The use of this principle is one of the ways the church helps bridge the gap between society's needs and the availability of resources. Rather than follow the traditional method of seeking contributions of canned food or money to purchase food, as often is the practice by agencies and other churches that assist in this way, the church's strategy is to obtain food at a much lower cost. To do so, it has approached canneries in Oregon's Willamette Valley and asked to buy canned vegetables with cans dented in the production process at the actual cost of manufacture. (The products inside the cans are not affected by damage, but the cans are unsuitable for sale at normal market prices.) The savings is remarkable, yet the quality unchanged, allowing for a greater quantity at the same cost.

Meat normally is in short supply for the relief agencies and children's homes. A concentrated effort is made by the church to provide large quantities of ground beef for their needs. The beef for this purpose is raised on Dr. Pamplin's farms near Sherwood, Oregon. Beef cattle there graze on grass and clover hay, and are fed only small amounts of grain. Beef fattened this way produces a leaner meat than that which is intensely grain-fed in the conventional manner. Yet when the entire animal (except for the choicest primal cuts) is ground into hamburger, the resulting meat is low in fat, tender and highly nutritious. Since meat is the primary protein source at the agencies and children's homes, this use of innovative economics allows Christ Community Church to provide considerably greater nutrition value at a significant cost savings.

A second ministry of Christ Community Church is sponsorship of a series of one-minute radio profiles called "One Who Believed," produced by staff writer Thomas K. Worcester and Dr. Robert B. Pamplin, Jr.

These mini-biographies dramatically describe the life of practicing Christians, living and deceased, and the impact faith had on their lives. The programs have been broadcast on both secular and Christian radio stations, with well-deserved listenership on each.

Many of the subjects of the broadcast were – or are – prominent individuals whose accomplishments have made them of interest as a story. Others are individuals who may not be well known, yet their story is remarkable. But, a consistent theme is deep, Christian faith central to the life of the subject, whether through a miraculous happening or conversion, or a strengthening of beliefs started early.

Some of the personalities profiled include Eddie Rickenbacker, George Washington, Mother Teresa, Jesse Owens, Isaac Newton, Ethel Waters, George Washington Carver, Clara Barton, Eric Liddell, David Livingstone, and Daniel Webster and others.

Many of their biographies follow.

BABE RUTH

"The One They Called Babe"

I t is quite possible that one name will always come up whenever folks gather to talk about the great stars of professional baseball: George Herman Ruth, better known as Babe Ruth.

Even without a candy bar to carry his name, the Babe would have been remembered. For this was the man who with the swing of a bat could – and did – change the fate of a game. Babe was an outstanding pitcher, yet it was his long-standing records for homeruns that put him in the Baseball Hall of Fame. Before Roger Maris and Hank Aaron rewrote the record books, Babe held claim to both the most home runs in a single season and for a career. Each record lasted several decades.

It also is possible that we might never have heard of Ruth had it not been for Brother Matthias at St. Mary's Industrial School in Baltimore, the place where Babe was reared. St. Mary's was a training school for orphans, incorrigibles, delinquents and runaways picked up on the streets of Baltimore. Babe qualified for admittance under the category of "incorrigible," though he hardly knew his parents. His early youth had been spent living over his father's saloon in Baltimore, and when he wasn't over the saloon he was in it, soaking up the atmosphere. Babe once commented that he didn't think he knew the difference between right and wrong during his boyhood.

So, Babe eventually landed at St. Mary's, where strict

regimen and continual religious training were the foundation of the program. Discipline alone might not have straightened Babe out, but the combination of discipline and introduction to a power over and above man registered with Babe. He was able to change.

Brother Matthias not only introduced Babe to religious training, but he recognized that Babe had more than average skills hitting, catching and throwing a baseball. He spent hours with Babe, bunting or hitting long fly balls to Babe, correcting the young man's mistakes as they went along. Brother Matthias was an impressive figure, standing 6 feet 6 inches and weighing 250 pounds, mostly muscle. He was not the kind of man even a tough street kid such as Babe could ignore had he wanted to.

Ruth spent more than a decade at St. Mary's, and left there in 1914 to begin a professional baseball career with the Baltimore Orioles. He went to the Boston Red Sox later that year, and found immediate success as a pitcher. But, by the time Babe was traded to the New York Yankees, in 1920, he was played regularly in the outfield.

It would be a misnomer to think that Babe Ruth was the fabled paragon of virtue when he left St. Mary's. He wasn't. With the restrictions off, Babe really began to cut capers. As Babe once wrote:

"I strayed from the church, but don't think I forgot my religious training. I just overlooked it. I prayed often and hard, but, like many irrepressible young fellows, the swift tempo of my living shoved religion into the background."

Ruth's game reached full stride in the pin-striped uniform of the New York Yankees. In 1927 he hit 60 home runs, a record that lasted until 1961. When the Yankees built a new stadium, it quickly was named "the House That Ruth Built."

In addition to making a name for himself at home plate, Babe Ruth did much to popularize baseball, especially among the youngsters who idolized him. Some of his critics thought it just a publicity stunt for Babe to spend so much time with the children who came to the various ball parks in which he played, but Babe didn't mind the criticism. He never forgot where he came from, and in every grubby-faced kid he saw another useful citizen if someone – perhaps someone like a Brother Matthias – just gave him a chance. Babe cared a lot about those kids. Enough to comment how he felt about early religious training:

"The more I think about it, the more important I feel it is to give kids 'the works' as far as religion is concerned. They'll never want to be holy – they'll act like tough monkeys in contrast, but somewhere inside will be a solid little chapel. It may get dusty from neglect, but the time will come when the door will be opened with much relief. But the kids can't take it if we don't give it to them."

To be sure, Babe was speaking from experience. His own "solid little chapel" got very dusty from neglect as he enjoyed life to the fullest. If Babe had one regret in later years concerning his playing days and the example he set for youth, it could be that it was that he might have let kids down when he forgot – or ignored – some of the rules of life. Though he did not participate regularly in church services, Babe had what he considered his personal altar in New York, a big window overlooking the city's lights. There he often would kneel in prayer, asking God to help him not make a fool of himself and to measure up to what He expected of Babe. It was a time when Babe felt quite humble.

Babe was inducted into the Baseball Hall of Fame in 1936, an honor that caught the attention of the world. And, when Babe died of cancer in 1948, he again was in the headlines, for this popular sports hero could not escape such attention. But, George Herman Ruth – the man named Babe – was quietly inducted into an even greater Hall of Fame as he passed from one life to another, for Babe was one who believed.

EDDIE RICKENBACKER

"Beyond Medals"

C aptain Eddie Rickenbacker is well known in
military circles for his daring exploits as a World
War I flying ace and winner of the Congressional Medal
of Honor.

What is not as well known about Rickenbacker, former
president of Eastern Airlines, is an incident in World War
II that led to his declaration of faith and his determination to serve God as best he could.

It happened in October, 1942. Captain Rickenbacker
was on a special mission for Secretary of War Henry L.
Stimpson. He was to leave California in a B17 Flying
Fortress to deliver a secret message to General Douglas
MacArthur, who then was in Australia. As the aircraft
gained speed down the runway on takeoff, a tire blew
out, bringing the big plane to a jarring halt. Unknown to
the aircraft's crew, that abrupt stop disturbed the B17's
sensitive navigational instruments. Repairs were made,
and the plane took off for Canton Island, the first
refueling stop.

As the flight approached the spot where the navigator's
instruments showed the island to be, the men saw no
land. Only the vast blue of the Pacific Ocean stretched
out below the aircraft. The crew made radio contact with
Canton Island, but since the island personnel had no
direction-finding equipment, they could not give a
reference course for landing. The pilot began flying a

search pattern for the island, maintaining a heading for a few miles, then changing course. But, the aircraft's fuel ran out before the island was sighted. As the plane descended toward the ocean, the radio operator issued an urgent "May Day." The message went unheard.

The plane crashed in the water. The eight men aboard tumbled into the aircraft's three small liferafts, which were roped together, but which lacked any food or water except four small oranges Rickenbacker had grabbed as they left the plane. For several days the men were blistered by the sun, starved, and soon covered with open running sores as a result of exposure to the sea water. Rain squalls provided a meager amount of drinking water, captured by wringing the moisture out of their clothes. But the precious water was scant, and had to be rationed.

One of the men carried with him a copy of the New Testament, so the group started each morning and ended each evening with a prayer and Bible reading. At first this was difficult for some of the cynics and nonbelievers in the group, for their hardships were nearly intolerable and no relief or rescue came. But, on the morning of the eighth day adrift, a half-dazed Eddie Rickenbacker felt something land on his head. As if by premonition he knew it was a seagull. Slowly, very cautiously, he reached up and grabbed the bird by its feet. The men killed and divided the bird, eating its tough meat and small bones raw. They then used its entrails for fish bait, soon catching enough fish to begin the chain of survival so desperately needed. Through the heaven-sent sacrifice of the lone bird, hundreds of miles from land, seven of the eight men were able to sustain themselves until their rescue 16 days later near the Ellice Islands, about 500 miles southwest of Canton Island. One crew member died at sea.

Eddie Rickenbacker lost more than one-third of his body weight in the ordeal, but found through his suffering and facing death the meaning of God. It was clear to Eddie Rickenbacker, one who believed, that God had kept Eddie alive to serve Him. Prayer had been answered.

GEORGE WASHINGTON

"Touched by Destiny"

"H is integrity was almost pure, his justice the most inflexible I have ever known...

"He was indeed, in every sense of the words, a wise, a good and a great man... on the whole, his character was, in its mass, perfect... it may truly be said, that never did nature and fortune combine more perfectly to make a man great..."

These were the words of Thomas Jefferson, written in praise of his friend, George Washington, after Washington's death on December 14, 1799. Washington was revered not only by words; his name appears on a multitude of schools, cities, streets, counties, buildings and parks, and the nation's capitol honors him. He also is the only president to have a state named for him.

How – and why – did George Washington achieve such prominence? Is it just destiny that caused the discovery of this good and great man at a time when his nation needed crucial leadership?

Nothing in Washington's early years would indicate that this man was touched by such a destiny. Born on Pope's Creek Farm, in Westmoreland County, Virginia, he spent most of the early years on a largely undeveloped plantation on the Potomac River that later became Mount Vernon. His only playmates were his brothers and sisters, for the nearest neighbor was several miles away. But young George apparently enjoyed roaming the woods and helping with the farm chores. George was nearly seven years old when the family moved again, this time to the 260-acre Ferry Farm, across the Rappahannock River from Fredericksburg, Virginia.

Accurate records concerning George Washington's education do not exist, but he seemed to have no more than seven or eight years of formal education. His favorite subject was mathematics, leading to a career as a surveyor when he was but 15 years old. He also learned to write well, and to keep good business records, and during the rest of his life he kept diaries and accurate accounts of income and expenses.

Washington assisted with the management of the Ferry Farm, learning farming skills and techniques that helped him later in his recess from public life. He also developed firm religious beliefs and concentrated on standards of behavior that he felt would be useful to him. As a youth, he was described as attentive, dependable, sober, quiet and dignified.

Washington's mother squelched an early desire for him to enter the British Royal Navy when she would not give him permission to enlist as a 14-year-old. But, by the time George was 20 his interest in the military had become strong, and though he had no training or experience, he was given a commission in the Virginia militia and assigned to training of new recruits. He quickly became accomplished in military tactics and affairs.

Washington rose rapidly through military ranks as the drums of war began beating in earnest in the Ohio Valley and the Atlantic seaboard, where the French and the British vied not only for land but for the support of the American colonists. When orders from London threatened to lower his rank from colonel to captain, he resigned his commission and returned to the farm.

Washington soon was called back to service and received recognition as an astute field commander as his raw troops engaged French forces. He also learned that the British troops moved slowly and that they could be beaten – factors that became important later when he accepted the position of leadership in the Continental Army.

From the mid-1750s until his retirement, the career of George Washington was one of command and leadership – and of firsts. Involved from the beginning in the broiling revolution against the British crown, he took part in the meetings of the Continental Congress, and was unanimously elected first commander in chief of the newly-formed Continental Army that eventually defeated the British at Yorktown, after much suffering and anguish by General Washington and his troops. Washington prayed through the bitter winters from 1775 to 1780 when his soldiers were cold and hungry and their trail could be traced by blood in the snow from bare and torn feet. But, Washington's faith carried over to his troops and to the nation, moving this ragged band of patriots to victory and American independence.

Washington rejected a movement to establish a new monarchy with him as king of the Colonies, and instead returned to his Virginia home. But, five years later he was back in the thick of politics as first president of the Constitutional Convention, called in 1787 to replace the weak Articles of Confederation and establish the document that united the new American states. Though he took little part in debates over the document, Washington held the convention together until the Constitution was drafted. A year later, when enough states had approved the Constitution so that the government could be formed, he was elected President of the United States by representatives at the electoral college.

Perhaps George Washington's faith can best be shown by this statement from his first inaugural address:

"In tendering this homage to the great Author of every public and private good, I assure myself that it expressed your sentiments not less than my own; nor those of my fellow citizens at large, less than either. No people can be bound to acknowledge and adore the invisible Hand, which conducts the affairs of men, more than the people of the United States. Every step by which they have advanced to the character of an independent nation seems to have been distinguished by some token of Providential agency."

George Washington, one who believed, was touched by that invisible Hand more than others.

ETHEL WATERS

"The Joy of Giving"

To Ethel Waters, singer and actress who enthralled audiences for nearly 50 years with a remarkable career on stage and screen, one of the greatest pleasures of life was the joy of giving.

Miss Waters gave liberally. Not only did she impart immense pleasure to the theater goers who witnessed her performances, but also a great sharing of love. To many she was "Mom." Though she had no children by birth, she had many to whom she was a mother in every sense of the word.

Miss Waters was seen live in theater and concert, and in motion pictures and on television, to the delight of millions. It might be lesser known, however, that she also was a regular contributor to the Christian crusades of Billy Graham and others, performing gospel music and spirituals with a special richness that came from her own heritage. She had another gift that she shared, too. Blessed with a keen mind and the ability to develop meaningful thought, she was a valued speaker and conversationalist.

Ethel Waters had a favorite hymn, one that became virtually a trademark for her. It was "His Eye is on the Sparrow," and for many years she sang it with a meaning given by no other artist. To Ethel Waters, she was the sparrow that God had touched.

A large sparrow, to be sure. Amply structured, Miss

Waters at one time weighed 350 pounds, and while she could joke about her bulk, it limited her mobility and she often spent long hours self-confined in her apartment, finding it easier to stay home than go out.

Therein was the contrast that dogged this remarkable human being much of her adult life. To the public who saw and knew her, she was an ebullient, giving, loving person – which she was. Privately, she often was lonely, spending many hours in hotel rooms or suites. Even when home she sometimes did not seek out company for long periods of time. But, give her an audience, and Ethel Waters was at her best.

What were the forces that shaped the life of Ethel Waters? Born illegitimately and in poverty of a 12-year-old mother who had been raped at knife-point, she was raised primarily by her grandmother and aunts, though she spent much of her childhood living in red-light districts of Philadelphia and Camden where housing was barely affordable. A large child, Ethel also was quick-minded and tough. In situations that she couldn't talk her way out of, she usually could fight her way. She became an excellent judge of character at a young age, knowing a scam or a con when she saw it and often labeling it as such. (This early training assisted her as an adult, where she quickly could judge people who truly were her friends and those who wished to use her.) She also developed life-long abstinence from alcohol and drugs, for she had witnessed their horrors in the ghetto.

While Ethel's schooling was spotty, she learned rapidly, for she had a superior intellect and absorbed knowledge easily. Oddly, the one thing she did not learn was to read music, even though her stage career initially was as a singer and she continued to perform musically nearly to the time of her death.

One factor she desperately missed in her young

childhood was the true demonstration of affection. To her mother she was a constant reminder of the worst moment of her life. Even the grandmother she called Mom did not *show* love for Ethel, and the youngster built her defense mechanisms accordingly. Thus Ethel was not prepared for the genuine love and concern expressed for her when she began attending a Catholic school, where her nun teachers were captivated by her innate charm and skills. Gradually Ethel learned to return the warmth and affection.

Not only did Ethel change her behavior, but she opened her mind and her heart to God. As her ghetto behavior tamed, her search for a closer relationship with God intensified. She learned to pray and maintained an honesty that sometimes even shocked the parish priest.

Ethel was ecumenical, though. It was at a Methodist Quarterly Meeting in Chester, Pennsylvania, at the age of twelve that she believed "God touched this sparrow." From that time on she found something to which she could cling. And share.

As is well known, Ethel Waters went on to a brilliant career as a singer and actress. Acclaimed by critics and nominated for untold awards for her performances, she thrilled millions over the years, all the time enlarging her "family." Prayer was an important element of her life, though Ethel claimed she really didn't pray – just had an ongoing conversation with her precious Jesus.

In her later years, when Ethel Waters' performances were mostly at crusades, it was said that she never really left show business, just changed her message. Perhaps so. But one thing is known. Ethel Waters, blessed with the talent she was willing to share at almost all cost, also was blessed with another gift: brilliant, spontaneous thought which she often shared best at Christian witness to the God she loved and served.

JOAB POWELL

"Only Good Things Count"

The huge man in the black, home-spun coat raised a massive fist and the words exploded:

"I am the Al-pha and the O-Me-gah – the beginning and the end. For the righteous there is no escapin' the love of the Lord, and for the sinful there is no escapin' His punishin' hand. I am preachin' to convert the sinners and to keep the feet of the converted from slippin'."

It was Joab Powell, 300 pounds of frontier preacher, extolling his beliefs to followers in Oregon territory. And Joab Powell – or Uncle Joab as he was called – needed no special sanctuary to confine his booming voice or sacramental objects to confirm his faith. Whether on a stump, under a tree or in a schoolhouse, Uncle Joab answered his call, and the Oregon settlers came from miles around to hear him preach the gospel as only Powell could.

For all his size and bluster, Joab Powell was a simple man following a simple theology: "Only good things count." But the way he delivered that message was what impressed his listeners. He could fix an eye on a wary subject and heaven help the man if he *were* a sinner. Uncle Joab would send him away properly chastised.

It is not known for certain whether or not Powell could write his name, but it is known that he could not read. Though born of Tennessee Quaker stock, Joab's family had become Baptists on the early frontier. Their theology was strictly Calvinistic, yet the individualism and spirit of the frontier often established a belief in free will and the innate goodness of man. So it was with Joab.

Powell's education was in the fields and forests, for he had no schooling. He joined the church in 1824, and was moved by the words "Go ye into all the world and preach the gospel to every creature." His uncomplex mind accepted the words literally, and he followed. Joab had married a German girl when he was only 19 years old, though she spoke little English and he no German. Yet she developed a good command of the language, and became his Biblical "teacher." Every evening, Mrs. Powell would read from the Bible, slowly, often repeating and rereading verses as Joab accepted them to memory. He memorized an entire hymn book the same way and when he began active preaching he laced his sermons with frequent song.

Joab began that preaching after the family moved to Missouri in 1830 and settled near Independence, a few miles from the eastern terminus of the Oregon Trail. Joab often preached in the shade of a huge walnut tree, which became known locally as "Joab's pulpit." When he wasn't exhorting crowds to sidestep sin, Joab farmed to put bread on his own table.

Caught up in the fever to move west, Joab eventually took his family by wagon to Oregon's Willamette Valley, settling near the Santiam River. Following his practice in Missouri, he mixed preaching and farming, with his specialty being the revival meetings he conducted up and down the valleys of the Willamette River and its tributaries. Though the land was sparsely populated, crowds turned out to hear Uncle Joab, and he is believed to have baptized nearly 3,000 followers.

Joab lived the life he preached. A man of piety, he found the good in all people. His style was unique in its informality: Saint Peter and Saint Paul were "General Peter and General Paul" to Joab, and he took other liberties with names and deeds. But always his theme was singular: "Only good things count," and regardless of how the message was formed, this was the belief that directed his life and that which Powell expected others to accept. All the time he flayed sin he had the capacity to make friends of the sinners.

Joab Powell always preached kindness, especially to those who were less fortunate. An ardent abolitionist, he also advocated kindness to Indians, a feeling hardly universal on the frontier. And, Uncle Joab never had any fixed charge for his preaching. He asked only for board and lodging and hay for his horse when he was away from home, though with his prodigious appetite that fee sometimes seemed high between harvests. If a congregation offered him any compensation he would take it. At the close of a meeting, when he rode away from the home of a willing host, he would shout, "Just charge my bill to the Lord."

Joab Powell also was a fine judge of character, and used humor effectively in his preachings. Once, while acting as chaplain for the Oregon Legislature, he offered this invocation:

"Lord, forgive them, for they know not what they do!"

Joab Powell, one who believed, died in 1872, two years after his beloved wife passed on. The inscription he dictated for her tombstone read: "There remaineth therefore a rest to the people of God." Uncle Joab, pioneer, preacher and farmer, had duly earned that same rest.

JESSE OWENS

"Pray, J.C.... Pray"

The five-year-old sharecropper's son knew he was dying. His mother had removed the large lump from his scrawny chest with a kitchen knife two days before, and now the family was gathered in the cabin they called home rather than working the fields. His shirt and the sack-cloth bedclothes were soaked with blood.

On the third night, in moments when he was awake from the daze his life had become, he heard his father praying outside the door of the cabin. Slowly, painfully, the child dragged himself to the doorway.

When his father realized young James Cleveland Owens was there, he gathered him in his arms and said, "Pray, J.C.... pray."

Though the child did not know what to pray, father and son clasped each other. The confused youngster wanted only that the bleeding and hurt stop. The father prayed that a life be spared.

When Owens and his son returned to the cabin, the bleeding had stopped. And the child who survived that crisis on the Alabama farm grew up to become one of America's most famous athletes, Jesse Owens, once dubbed the world's fastest human being.

Today an athlete with the skills and accomplishments of a Jesse Owens would be inundated with lucrative endorsements and contracts. Fame and fortune would be his. Jesse Owens had the fame, but had promises, not fortune, when he reached the height of his career at the 1936 Olympics in Berlin, Germany.

But that gets ahead of his story.

After young J.C. Owens' life was spared, his father decided to take his family north to Cleveland, Ohio, where he hoped to give his children the opportunities he never had had. Grandson of a Negro slave, Henry Owens knew only sharecropping and debt, and the only way his family could have food was when all the children worked in the fields, too. Their lot was not a meaningful life, merely a bare existence.

Yet even then, when the family walked the nine miles home from church, little J.C. would talk about "going to college,"– words that he had heard, though he didn't know what they meant.

After the family moved to Cleveland, Henry Owens worked at odd jobs when he could find them and his wife and older daughter worked as maids. The older boys toiled as part-time janitors or unloading freight cars, and even J.C., youngest of the ten children, brought home a dollar a week hauling groceries and cleaning a greenhouse. Together they survived, though the older children dropped out of school one-by-one to assist with the family income. Henry Owens, who could neither read nor write, had the hardest time getting good jobs, a fact that ate at his soul.

Life began changing for J.C. the year he entered fifth grade. His school, a racially-mixed elementary, was near a high school and the high school coach taught the physical education classes for the younger grades. One day Coach Charles Riley asked J.C. if he would like to be on the track team when he got to high school. Riley had spotted something in the spindly youngster who often out-distanced his classmates in the P.E. class games. Riley also mispronounced J.C.'s name, for he had heard it as

"Jesse," not "J.C..." But the boy liked the new name, and informed his family that from then on he was to be Jesse.

Riley had the boy work out before school since his after-school jobs prevented Jesse from training then. Three years later, thin Jesse had matured into a muscular athlete who began winning races with regularity, though he suffered humiliating losses at first. But Coach Riley not only taught Jesse how to win but how to lose. He also planted the idea that Jesse could run in the Olympics.

Jesse Owens struggled to become the best runner he could. Upon the advice of Coach Riley he turned down college scholarship offers and worked his way through Ohio State. Along the way he kept up the courtship of the girl he'd met years ago when he first came to Cleveland, who became his bride. And Jesse ran faster and faster, and jumped farther and farther. By the time of the 1936 Olympics, Owens held the world records in the 100 and 200-yard dashes and the broad jump.

The Berlin Olympics were more than just athletes from each country gathering to perform at their best. Adolph Hitler now was in power in Germany fomenting hate for anyone other than his Aryan "supermen." Jesse Owens, particularly, was a target of his wrath, and one Hitler felt his superb German athletes would defeat.

But Jesse didn't just win at Berlin. He astounded the world, taking gold medals in 100 and 200-meter dashes, the 400-meter relay and the broad jump. In the latter event he was encouraged by a man who became a firm friend, German champion Luz Long. Jesse Owens clearly outran Hitler.

Though Jesse Owens had gone to church as a youngster and had accepted the Christian faith as part of his life, it wasn't until years after his Olympic victories that he truly found internal peace through the acceptance of Christ. Using the fame of his name and the will of his

God, Jesse Owens traveled throughout the land in support of programs that aided the moral and physical development of America's youth. For Jesse Owens, one who believed, saw that as the way he could repay those who had helped him jump all the way from the Alabama sharecrop farm to the top of Mount Olympus.

JONI EARECKSON

"Refusing to Give Up"

J oni Eareckson's life can only be described as one of inspiration and determination.

When Joni was just 17 years old, a tragic diving accident left her paralyzed from the neck down. An active girl who had enjoyed and excelled at athletics, Joni suddenly found herself trapped inside a body without movement. She was so helpless she could not even wipe away the tears that came frequently as she considered her fate. Joni knew her entire way of living had changed.

For a year, Joni was confined to a hospital, where she was totally dependent on doctors, nurses and orderlies as she suffered through the pain of surgery and the indignity of bedsores. Completely immobile, Joni lay among other patients who existed in a zombie-like state, waiting to die. Her world consisted of catheter tubes and urine bags, and at times her spirits were so bleak even Joni would have welcomed the relief of death.

The one thing Joni had not given up on was her resolute faith in God. She continued to believe that through Him, all things worked out for the best. She placed total trust in God. It was this steadfast faith that helped her endure agonizing hours of physical therapy, treatment that led many to hopeless despair because of the pain and frustration.

For Joni, the therapy was a long, gradual process. Remarkably, her back muscles were retrained to the point that she could raise and lower her arms and operate an electric wheel chair. She even taught herself to write and draw with a pencil or brush clutched between her teeth. Determined to be as independent as possible, given her physical limitations, Joni developed her skills as an artist into a commercial craft displaying considerable talent.

Because of her dependence on God and an attitude that insured a bright future, Joni has been an inspiration to millions who have become familiar with her story. A book concerning her life was an internationally best seller and was followed by a motion picture about courageous Joni Eareckson, one who believed, who refused to give up.

GEOFFREY STUDDERT KENNEDY

"A Queer Instrument of God's Purpose"

H istory has not recorded the name of the British
foot soldier who tagged Church of England chaplain Geoffrey Studdert Kennedy with the nickname
"Woodbine Willie." But history has recorded that
Kennedy, both as Geoffrey Studdert Kennedy and as
Woodbine Willie was one of the most remarkable men
of the cloth of modern times.

A profile of Kennedy strings a necklace of contra-
dictory pearls. Small in stature, with sad eyes, a narrow
face elongated by early balding, bat-like ears consciously
oversized, he commanded no interest or respect with his
physical being. Yet when he opened his mouth, whether
with the eloquence of the university-trained lecturer or
the Irish "jarvie" of his heritage, people knew this
booming voice was not that of just another preacher.

That Kennedy was unconventional in his style is pure
understatement. He captured audiences with the skill of
a polished showman, but held them with word ropes that
displayed a depth of knowledge owned by few men, yet
thoughts that were explained in the simplest of words. He
was a master at assessing an audience and providing
exactly what they needed to hear.

Studdert Kennedy's intellect was recognized early in
his life. His father once said of a very young Kennedy,
"His brain works so hard his head gets hot." School
chums were challenged by his far-reaching ideas, and

even his teachers were stretched to keep his intellect in control. Yet Kennedy was a humble soul, much more conscious of his failures than of his many successes.

Born into a lineage of Church of England clergy in 1883, he was one of nine children of the second wife of his father, the Rev. William Studdert Kennedy. Five other children had been born to Rev. Kennedy's first wife. Together this large, loving Irish family lived in Leeds, England, where Studdert Kennedy's father was vicar of St. Andrew's church, a parish in the steamy slums of Leeds.

It was in these formative years that Studdert Kennedy became acutely aware of man's social needs; a problem that he later confronted as freely as he did his parishioners spiritual needs. Educated in a private grammar school and then Trinity College, Dublin, young Kennedy could readily translate Greek poetry into perfect English sentences. Yet his school contemporaries considered him a wild Irishman who used theatrical language or Irish dialect readily. But those who knew him best recognized the intellectual abilities that lay behind his oddities. Upon graduation from Trinity College in 1905, he started teaching in Calday Grammar School in Cheshire. Outwardly he seemed happy, but inwardly he was troubled with new ideas and thoughts, and mostly with the nagging decision of whether to follow his father, grandfather and two brothers into the ministry. This also was a period of vigorous, disordered reading for Studdert, a habit he had gained as a child.

Studdert Kennedy entered Ripon Clergy College in 1907, and was ordained one year later, going into a world then considered a wild, spiritual desert, with lean times ahead in the ministry. Kennedy was aware of enormous social injustice, cruel class divisions and political ferment when ordained at the Cathedral of Worcester and took up his ministry at the Rugby Parish Church.

Kennedy's biographer, William Purcell, notes that Studdert dropped into the Rugby parish "like a bomb." He struck many as being wild and undisciplined, and to others he seemed foolish. But, as a curate at Rugby he was described by his vicar as being "an Irishman with brains, infinite charm, devotion to his work, a fine sense of humor, but of an undisciplined mind." Not a week would pass when Kennedy would storm the vicarage with another thought-provoking idea, sometimes based upon his own sorting out of theologic considerations, sometimes based upon direct needs of his people.

Kennedy was entirely eccentric as to clothing and money, neither of which had any real meaning to him. His landlady finally kept his meager church earnings and doled out funds to him as an allowance, and even bought him clothes – until he gave away a new overcoat that she had provided him because he had found a man who was old and cold, with a greater need than his. Such was the immediacy of Kennedy's ministry. Often he would wear rags under his cassock. (Twenty years later, when he had become an important national figure in Great Britain, he went to a stately service at Westminster Abbey wearing football shorts under the scarlet robes of royal chaplain.)

Kennedy took over the slum district of Rugby parish, and often wandered into the pubs, where he could talk easily to the working man. He also preached on street corners, and he developed a "Babies' service" on Sunday afternoon when he could be found surrounded by young children, telling stories, singing songs and lighting birthday candles. At heart he was crudely sentimental. Above all he was known for concern for the down-trodden and his eloquence. Whenever Studdert was in the pulpit, the congregation swelled in numbers as people came from near and far to hear his words, delivered in his unorthodox style that sometimes included swearing. For all he offended – and he did offend many – hundreds more heard his message.

Studdert Kennedy first accepted his nation's cause when the drums of war sounded over Flanders, and he encouraged young men to join the army. He himself volunteered, and in 1915 was sent to France. His first service to the British Expeditionary Forces was delivered to 400 men in a muddy open field on Christmas morning, 1915, near Rouen. For the next several months he met every troop train going up to the front or returning, slogging through rain and mud for hours to pass out cigarettes – woodbines – and New Testaments, quick words of comfort and prayer, writing letters home for the weary soldiers, trying to cover the fear of battle with the mantle of Christ's love. Soon the legend of Woodbine Willie spread through the forces in France.

That Kennedy touched the minds and hearts of thousands of Brits at home and in the trenches is undeniable. Yet throughout the war he was haunted by the question of a young officer, wounded and hospitalized, who had asked: "What is God like? To me he still is the unknown God." Kennedy attempted to answer that question in poems, *Rough Verses* as he called them, written between shellings at the front.

Studdert Kennedy completely changed his view of the war during the four years he served as chaplain, returning home with a hatred for the carnage and waste of young lives. The asthma that had plagued him since childhood was worse, and the priest had only ten years to attempt to find solutions to the theological questions that burned in his intellect. A genuine hero whose fame brought out huge crowds each time he took to the speaker's stand or pulpit, Woodbine Willie still was more comfortable taking the word of God to the man on the street – his own special kind of preaching.

So absent-minded that he is reported to have left behind tooth brushes and pajamas all over England, and frequently missed important engagements because he forgot, Studdert Kennedy usually committed long sermons and talks to memory with just one writing. So well planned and polished were his talks that they seemed completely extemporaneous, for he spoke without notes and often included much anecdotal material. Of those patrons most affected by Kennedy were what William Purcell called the "floating voters of religion, who, if faced with a voting card for or against belief in God, would tend to place their cross in the affirmative square and then wonder wistfully if it were true. In any age there are people who will flock to that particular shepherd whose voice they seem to know, calling to them in their own half-sad, half-humorous accents. Geoffrey's was such a voice."

The noted William Temple, archbishop of Canterbury, regarded his contemporary, Studdert Kennedy, as simply "The finest priest I have ever known."

Yet Kennedy, one who passionately believed, described by Purcell as "a queer instrument of God's purpose," went to his grave in March, 1929, believing he had failed. But Woodbine Willie had failed only himself.

SAMUEL F.B. MORSE

"Of Dots and Dashes"

I f necessity is the mother of invention, then adversity is its aunt. At least one might believe so when considering why Samuel F. B. Morse provided the world with the telegraph in the mid-1800s.

Morse, a graduate of Yale University and promising portrait artist, had gone to England to study under British masters Washington Allston and Benjamin West. But, the young man was homesick, and dismayed that it took weeks for messages to get across the ocean by mail. For years he wished he could do something about that time lag.

Back in America, he established himself as a painter of considerable talent, and won recognition with his portraits of President James Monroe and French General Lafayette. He founded the National Academy of Design in 1825, and was its first president. As fame came to Morse, he went to Italy to study the works of the old masters and perfect his own technique. It was this trip that changed his entire career, and gave us one of the most noteworthy inventions of all time.

Morse was returning home on the liner *Sully* in 1832 when conversation in the dining saloon turned to recent discoveries in electricity and magnetism. Morse began to ponder electric circuits, and the ability to transmit intelligible electric signals over long distances. He spent the rest of the voyage filling his sketchbook with notes, figures and drawings, attempting to devise a way to make electrical signals that could be sent from one place to another.

Morse returned home to numerous commissions for portraits and the assurance of a rewarding future, a far cry from the often impoverished artist. But, something other than art burned inside Samuel Morse, and he turned away from his painting and secreted himself in a small workshop.

For several lean years he worked on his theory, subjecting himself to ridicule and obscurity. He lived alone in the workshop, occasionally cooking a small amount of food for sustenance. When totally deprived of resources he would put aside the invention to earn a little money with his paint brushes, most of which he quickly spent on his scientific endeavor.

By 1836 Morse had a working model of the telegraph. A year later he applied for a patent for the American Electro Magnetic Telegraph, but even with patent in hand, the invention was not considered practical by either government officials or businessmen. If anything, Morse was ridiculed as a madman for thinking he could send messages by electricity. Demonstrations in Washington accomplished nothing, nor was the idea considered practical in England, France or Russia.

Five more years of discouragement followed, but Samuel Morse persevered. Finally, in 1843, Congress appropriated funds for an experimental telegraph line. An official test of Morse's invention required that a message be sent from Washington to Baltimore and returned correctly to Washington. Thus on May 24, 1844, Samuel Morse readied himself in the Supreme Court Room in Washington, while in Baltimore, a loyal assistant named Vail waited for the transmission.

On signal, Samuel F. B. Morse transmitted a series

of dots and dashes with his device, and back from Baltimore came the exact historic words: "What hath God wrought!" The telegraph was a success.

It is appropriate that Morse's message was a phrase from Scripture, for the artist-inventor was a devout Christian who gave credit to God for using him as an instrument in the discovery. Morse received many awards, medals, honorary distinctions and great wealth from the telegraph, yet he was to remark:

"I am not indifferent to the rewards of earth and the praise of my fellow men, but I am more pleased with the fact that my Father in heaven has allowed me to do something for Him and His world."

Years later, at a banquet in his honor, Morse again praised the source of his genius, noting "not unto us, but unto God be all the glory. Not what hath man, but what hath God wrought!"

Nor did Samuel Morse allow those convictions to stand as hollow quotes. Morse frequently made large contributions to churches, theological seminaries and missionary enterprises. In memory of his father, the Rev. Jedidiah Morse, he established a lectureship on the Relation of the Bible to the Sciences.

Ironically, it was at a tribute to the man who showed lightning to be electricity that Morse caught a fatal chill. He died April 2, 1872, following the outdoor unveiling of a statue of Benjamin Franklin in New York. Samuel F. B. Morse, one who believed, did not fear death when he passed on, for he was convinced of a life beyond mere mortality.

SGT. ALVIN YORK

"Trying Times for a Boy Like Me"

M onths before the noted World War I battle in which American hero Alvin York singlehandedly killed or captured more than 100 German soldiers, York told his commanding officer it was against his religion to kill.

How, then, did this gentle, humble man get into the position that made him a genuine hero and this country's most decorated soldier of the first World War? That is a story of conflict and principle not generally known.

Alvin York was born in the mountain country of northern Tennessee in 1887, in a little town called Pall Mall. His father was a hard-working farmer who also served as the town's blacksmith, and he passed on the work ethic to Alvin, one of 11 children.

But it was as a marksman that Alvin York became a local folk hero in Fentress County. A crack shot, he could hit dead center in a cross-shaped target carved in a tree from 100 yards away. It was this ability with the rifle that saved York and his fellow countrymen in the battle in France's Argonne Forest in 1918.

Though York's mother was a pious, God-fearing woman, Alvin did not share this virtue as a young man. In fact, he was much the opposite – a hard-drinking rounder who cared little for the ways of the Lord.

That was until Alvin York met Gracie Williams. Gracie, a well-bred Christian lass, told York that she would have nothing to do with him unless he changed his ways.

Her firmness, and her devout nature, coupled with the prayers for his salvation by York's mother, brought about an immediate – and lasting – conversion of the Tennesseean. At a small country church, Alvin York gave his life to Christ.

One of the convictions York accepted from his church was pacifism – total rejection of war and refusal to kill anyone for any reason. It was this belief that brought conflict to York when he received his draft notice in 1917, after the United States had been drawn into the war. His strong sense of duty would not allow him to sidestep responsibility to fight for his country, so he did not file as a conscientious objector. Yet he was very much aware of the sixth commandment, "Thou shalt not kill," and he wrote in his diary:

"Oh, those were trying times for a boy like me trying to live for God and do His blessed will."

York constantly amazed others with his rifle skills at training camp, but he also disturbed his superiors when he told them that "practicing to kill people is against my religion." Given leave to think about his status, York decided that duty to country and honor to God were not in conflict in time of war, and reported back to camp, ready to do whatever was needed of him.

The test came soon. In the Argonne Forest, York and 16 other Americans were scouting German positions when they surprised a German squad in camp and took 20 prisoners. As they were returning to their own lines with the prisoners, German machine guns opened fire, killing six of the Americans and wounding others. York was isolated from his squad. Calmly, one by one, York shot enemy soldiers that tried to survey the scene, using only one bullet for each. Eventually the Germans no longer wanted to challenge this incredible marksman, and surrendered their positions. York and his handful of men took 132 prisoners back to Allied lines. The Tennessee rifleman had killed 25 other soldiers, and had silenced 35 machine guns.

Though showered with attention and honors, Alvin York remained modest as to his achievement, considering the exploit to be a miracle. "I am a witness to the fact that God did help me out of that hard battle, for the bushes were shot off all around me and I never got a scratch. So you can see that God will be with you if you will only trust Him, and I say he did save me."

After the war, Sgt. York helped establish several schools in his Tennessee county homeland, and took speaking engagements to raise money for the schools, providing young people an opportunity that he had not had. And, remaining true to his convictions, Alvin York led a long and purposeful life until his death in 1964. A soldier of both God and country, Alvin York was one who believed.

BABE DIDRIKSON ZAHARIAS

"It's What You Do That Counts"

Her given name was Mildred, but few of the thousands who knew her or knew of her were aware of that appellation. To the world she was Babe – Babe Didrikson Zaharias – quite possibly the greatest female athlete ever to live.

Babe was a champion by the standards of scores, times and tape measures, and just as much a champion as a person. She loved life and she loved competition, and made the most of each.

A native of Texas, Babe Didrikson first gained national attention in the 1930s for her efforts in track and field. Babe set world records in the javelin throw, the high jump and the hurdles. She even won one national women's track championship all by herself. As the only entry from her team, she won five events and placed in three others to outscore all the other teams in the meet.

But Babe's efforts were not restricted to running, throwing and jumping in track and field. She also had distinguished herself on the softball field, played AAU basketball, and was a high roller at the bowling alley.

Babe lived and played by the rules of the game. She once said: "In the sports world you learn right off, if you didn't already know it, that once the competition starts, your creed can't help or hurt you. It's what you are and what you do that counts."

Babe Didrikson, who married professional wrestler

George Zaharias and tacked his last name onto hers, also was a practicing Christian. Not a church-going Christian, as she readily admitted, but one who had always prayed and who "went to God for spiritual muscle." As her life progressed, she needed that muscle more and more.

Despite the fact that she had been outstanding in track, basketball, baseball, bowling and could hit a mean tennis ball, it was golf that eventually attracted her more than any other sport.

Her first time with a club in her hand she drove farther and straighter off the tee than most of the men with whom she was playing, causing them to believe she had privately had golf lessons. Not Babe – that is just the way she was. A natural.

Because of previous professionalism in other sports, Babe was required to play as a professional golfer when she first started out, but she quickly learned there was no money in the game for tournament female golfers and finally had her amateur status reinstated. She played several years as an amateur in tournaments and exhibitions, winning just about everything in sight.

A climactic year for Babe Zaharias was 1947, when she won 15 straight tournaments before going into the British Women's Amateur Championship, which she was the first American to win. Not only did Babe win the tournament, but she was an outstanding goodwill ambassador for her country, and quickly had the once-partisan English crowd behind her.

After that highly successful year, Babe turned pro once again, partly to help found the Ladies Professional Golf Association that was being established to give more recognition and prize money to women golfers.

It was in 1948 that Babe first noticed the pain and swelling in her left side. Usually one to face problems directly, she put off checking it, as the pain would come and go. It never was bad enough to keep her out of tournaments or off the golf course. Nor did it stop her from stepping up for recognition in 1950 as the female athlete of the half century, an award richly deserved.

But by March, 1952, the pain was so bad that Babe finished a tournament and went directly to a hospital where doctors found a femoral hernia in the strangulated stage at the top of her left thigh. Surgery corrected the problem, and shortly Babe was back on the golf course.

By November she was in pain again and very tired most of the time. It wasn't until the following March that she checked in with Dr. William Tatum, in Beaumont, Texas, who confirmed what Babe herself thought. She had cancer.

A colostomy was performed on the active Babe on April 17, 1953. Though she feared the disease, she said:

"My idea has always been that whatever God intended for me in this life, I'd go along with."

Babe also made a promise to God that if she recovered, she would do everything in her power to get out and help in the fight against cancer.

By July, 3½ months after the colostomy, Babe Zaharias was back on the golf course, playing in the Tam O'Shanter Tournament. She didn't just enter – she played to win, because "that's the standard the public has come to judge me by."

And Babe kept her proimse to God. She made many appearances at fund raisers for cancer research, and visited cancer patients in hospitals until she, herself, lost the final round in the game of life in 1956. Babe Didrikson Zaharias, one who believed, was 42 years old when she died of cancer.

TOYOHIKO KAGAWA

"Traitor or Patriot of Peace?"

W hen Japanese Christian Toyohiko Kagawa died in
1960, his country's newspapers wrote long
eulogies praising his social work in the slums of Japan
and his long and untiring efforts toward world peace.

Yet Toyohiko Kagawa was the same man who many
times had been imprisoned as a traitor for his pacifist
beliefs during Japan's military aggression, and who had
incurred the wrath of both government officials and
industrialists for his efforts to reduce the effects of
poverty and to provide fair wages and hours for Japanese
factory and dock workers.

That he lived a life of conflict is not surprising. This
unswerving Christian in a Shinto and Buddhist land
took the teachings of Christ to heart in his life and his
deeds. In his lifetime he suffered beatings, fires, jailing,
and other indignities. Yet he was known throughout the
world for his efforts toward peace and social reform.

Kagawa was recognized early as one who stood for
what he believed, and who would not compromise his
positions for his own safety or comfort. He became
familiar with the words of Christ when he attended a
boarding school conducted by an American missionary,
where part of the English lessons were taught from the
New Testament. Kagawa saw in Christ a person he could
follow, and vowed to serve his own life as had the Master.
A brilliant student, he learned easily and usually was at

the top of his class in exams. He even taught himself German and French so that he could study the works of European scholars in their original language.

Kagawa met his first resistance from the forces of authority while a student at another school. Japan was at war with Russia at the time, and part of the instruction for all young men was compulsory military training. One day on the drill field Kagawa threw down his rifle, and declared that as a Christian he did not believe in war, and could not fight. When he refused orders to pick up the rifle, he was savagely kicked and beaten by the sergeant-major in charge. His classmates admired his courage, if not his judgment.

Later, as a college student in Tokyo, he was attacked by a group of fellow students after espousing pacifism. As his attackers left him, bloody and crumpled on the ground, Kagawa pulled himself to his knees and said: "God, forgive them." These simple words shocked and subdued the group, some of whom became close friends and converts to Christ as well.

Kagawa decided to train for the ministry while in school, forgoing a promising career as a scholar and teacher. But after two years in ministerial training at Kobe, his concerns for the poverty-stricken workers in the nearby slum of Shinkawa made him give up full time studies and move in to live with people who he felt he could help. In giving his decision to his professors at the college, Kagawa told them:

"I someday will become a minister, but I don't want to spend my life preaching to Christian people already in the church. I will go to those who aren't; the poor, the wicked, those who never have heard of Jesus Christ."

Some of his professors were relieved at his decision, for the young Kagawa had disturbed them with his beliefs that the government should be doing something about the slums, and that workers should have fair pay and reasonable hours. "A minister's job is to preach, not get mixed up in arguments about housing and wages," one said. Such thoughts did not suit the activist Kagawa.

At Shinkawa Kagawa lived among dock and factory workers barely feeding their families, as well as criminals, drug addicts, alcoholics, compulsive gamblers, and mentally ill turned out of their homes. The area had no proper sanitation, and medical facilities were out of reach. Though the conditions were worse than he had anticipated, Kagawa overcame the jibes of hecklers as he preached in the streets, and gradually began to see the effects of his work as more and more people came to hear his stories of Jesus and a different life that could be theirs. Though Kagawa had only a small hut for a home, a collection of beggars and other derelicts soon began moving in with him, accepting his food and care as if expected of him. With financial aid provided by the college officers who approved of his efforts, Kagawa rented three other huts which he rebuilt into a dormitory for his flock.

Even after he married, Kagawa continued to live in Shinkawa, and his bride soon learned to love the slum people, though like her husband, she hated the slum itself. Often she was caring for as many as 20 derelicts in their home. Kagawa also had become the spokesman for the workers, and met with industrialists to argue their case for better wages and working conditions. Though the businessmen disliked him for his work, they came to respect Kagawa for his beliefs.

Not so the military. As Kagawa became well-known throughout Japan for his writings and lectures, he was branded a traitor by the military for his unswerving pacifism. When Japanese armed forces invaded China in the 1930s, Kagawa toured America and China, preaching peace and apologizing for his country's militarism. At the time Kagawa learned of Japan's attack on Pearl Harbor on December 7, 1941, he and Christian friends in Riverside, California, were involved in a 24-hour prayer for peace. During the remainder of World War II Kagawa was imprisoned several times by military leaders who considered him a traitor to Japan's cause.

By then Kagawa had been established as one of his country's leading authorities on poverty and social reform. He had been heavily involved in the rebuilding of Tokyo after the disastrous earthquake of 1923, when, on his own, he went to the city and personally organized work crews and relief stations. As the city was being rebuilt, he convinced authorities to clear the slums, a policy that was adopted for Tokyo as well as several other major cities. Eventually he was asked to serve as head of Tokyo's welfare department, though he would accept no salary and would work only part-time, saying he needed half of each month for his preaching and personal care of the downtrodden.

Though hated by the militarists, disliked by the industrialists, and feared by government workers threatened by his calls for social reform, it was Kagawa who a year before the end of World War II was called upon by his government to head a committee being established to care for wartime homeless and refugees. After the Japanese surrender, Kagawa was summoned to the office of the Prime Minister, who asked his help in teaching the Japanese people how to love their enemy, as Christ had told his followers.

When General Douglas MacArthur assumed his position as supreme commander of occupied Japan, he sent for Kagawa, about whom he had heard many rumors and some truths. Expecting to meet a commanding figure befitting his reputation, MacArthur instead met an undistinguished elderly man in a simple suit, blind in one eye from a disease contracted at Shinkawa, his slight frame wracked by a long-ago bout with tuberculosis. But Kagawa's zeal impressed even the egocentric MacArthur. Kagawa convinced the general that the Japanese people were starving, and provided a plan to get food to the masses without the taint of blackmarket thefts, a startling performance in itself. Once again, Toyohiko Kagawa, one who believed, had served his suffering people, demonstrating that in his love for Christ he had dedicated his life to others, as he believed all Christians should do.

PETER MARSHALL

"A Voice in the Dark"

As a youngster in his native Scotland, Peter Marshall knew a life of deprivation. His father died when Peter was but four years old, causing the family to struggle just to obtain the bare essentials. When still a lad, Peter decided to learn about the sea, and he became a deck apprentice in the British Merchant Marine. But, a seaman's life was not to be for Peter Marshall, as a greater influence moved his heart to become a servant for Christ.

Peter worked one summer in the village of Bamburg, England, located in the Northumberland countryside. This is an area known for its limestone mines, fields of wheat and barley, pastures, and open moorland where sheep graze. While walking from a nearby village to Bamburg one night, Peter decided to take a shortcut across the moor. His only concern was that the path would take him near the deep pit of an abandoned limestone quarry.

The night was totally dark: no moon or stars penetrated a thick cloud cover to provide a comforting light on his treadway. The air was still. Only the occasional whirring wings of moor birds and the distant bleating of sheep disturbed the eerie quiet as Peter pushed through the moor with a confidence known only to youth. Suddenly, without forewarning, a voice called out in the darkness:

"Peter."

Peter stopped, and stammered, "W-who is there."

But, there was no response. Peter walked on, picking up his pace. Once again the same voice called out: "PETER!"

A startled Peter Marshall stopped completely, and as he did so, fell forward on his knees. Reaching out, Peter felt only space ahead of him. Slowly, without moving his body, he felt around him and discovered that he was on a narrow precipice high over the quarry pit. One more step forward or to the side and he would have fallen to certain death.

This incident had a profound effect on the young merchant seaman. He was certain in his mind that the voice he heard was that of God, saving him from death so that he could be of service to mankind. Peter subsequently decided to enter the ministry. Through the encouragement and assistance of his cousin, Peter immigrated to the United States. God's will directed him through several different jobs until the means were provided for Peter to enter Columbia Seminary in Decatur, Georgia.

Peter Marshall had a distinguished career in the pulpit, with his last pastorate that of New York Presbyterian Church in Washington, D.C. He also served as chaplain of the United States Senate from 1947 until his untimely death in 1949, at the age of 47, ending one of the truly influential ministries of this century.

DAVID LIVINGSTONE

"A Missionary, Heart and Soul"

H ad it not been for an enterprising New York newspaper editor, English-speaking folklore might have never have savored one of its favorite phrases: "Dr. Livingstone, I presume?"

That simple greeting came about when American journalist Henry M. Stanley greeted David Livingstone after a year's search in deepest Africa for the medical missionary in 1871-72. Stanley had been sent to Africa to find Livingstone by James Gordon Bennett, editor of the *New York World,* after the noted missionary had been reported murdered. Stanley's charge was to find Livingstone or his remains, but in any case to come back with a story. That he did!

Henry Stanley had little more than detached interest in David Livingstone when given the assignment by Bennett, though he was curious why the world press was making such a fuss over the presumed death of a missionary. But, as he read all he could about David Livingstone in preparation for his journey to Africa, he became fascinated. This is what he learned:

English-born David Livingstone had studied medicine and theology in the late 1830s in his native England, but before settling into a physician's career he answered another call that he felt God-given: the evangelization of Africa.

Dr. Livingstone arrived at the small South African

mission station directed by Robert Moffat in 1841, highly charged with the zeal to take the gospel to African masses. Livingstone and Moffat soon realized that both their efforts were not needed at the station, so the newcomer moved 250 miles north to extend the mission's influence in the beautiful Mabotsa Valley.

It was here that Dr. Livingstone had the first of many dangerous encounters. The village in Mabotsa was much troubled by lions, according to Livingstone's journal, and the missionary tried to help by shooting the beasts. But it was an act that nearly cost Livingstone his life, for he once was attacked and mauled by a lion he had wounded. Though his life was spared, his left arm was crushed, maiming him for life.

Undaunted, Livingstone continued his work at the Mabotsa station, aided by Mary Moffat, daughter of Robert Moffat, whom he married. Though a thoroughly masculine and fearless man, Livingstone was tender, and he found in Mary an ideal mate whom he loved with the same passion that he loved Africa. For the most part, his African subjects recognized and revered Livingstone for these feelings.

By 1850 David Livingstone felt God was calling him to the difficult task of opening up the interior of the Dark Continent. Many of his friends disagreed, saying he should stay in one place, preaching the gospel and seeking conversions with each service. Livingstone responded that if he followed only his *own* inclination he probably would settle down, but drawn by a higher wish, he and Mary set out for the interior of Africa.

The Livingstones reached Cape Town in 1852, not having found a suitable location for a mission station. Worse, David Livingstone realized that the fragile Mary could not endure arduous travel, for she had nearly died of fever on their long journey. Reluctantly, the Livingstones parted at Cape Town, Mary returning to England in April, 1852, to remain there until David had found a suitable mission location in central Africa.

With the Boer War between Dutch and English settlers in South Africa then in full swing, David Livingstone soon learned that he had been the subject of African village plunder by Boers who sought revenge for the natives' allowing an Englishman to live with them and to pass unmolested in the interior. Livingstone was both outraged and remorseful that the people to whom he had ministered had suffered, especially those who had not readily accepted Christ. The Boer attacks, instead of stopping him, merely made him more determined than ever to go deeper into Africa with his message.

Mary Livingstone rejoined her husband in 1859, in time to share with him the joy of seeing a mission that had been established in central Africa. Shortly though, not only did the mission fail, but Mary Livingstone died, nearly crushing the spirit of David, who had already endured many hardships. For the first time, David Livingstone indicated a willingness to die.

The missionary made his last visit to England in 1865, and when he returned to Africa the next year, he vanished into the interior. For the next five years he was not seen nor heard from, giving rise to the rumors that sent journalist Henry Stanley on his quest in 1871.

Stanley and his party searched for Livingstone for nearly a year, and with food and water becoming scarce were nearly ready to abandon the trip when they learned from a native caravan that an elderly white man had entered the Arab village of Ujiji. Stanley set out immediately for the village, arriving there in a few days. When he pushed through the crowds, he saw a "white man with a beard." Stanley wrote in his journal: "I…would have embraced him, only, he being an Englishman, I did not know how he would receive me: so I did what moral cowardice and false pride suggested was the best thing – walked deliberately to him, took off my hat and said: 'Dr. Livingstone, I presume?' 'Yes,' said he with a kind smile, lifting his cap slightly."

Stanley remained with Livingstone four months, learning that the missionary had suffered much in his five-year absence from civilization. He had survived numerous bouts with malaria, as well as pneumonia, starvation, and ambushes. Yet he recounted his trials without remorse, saying:

"I am a missionary, heart and soul. In (God's) service I wish to live; in it I wish to die. Viewed in relation to my calling – the end of my geographical feat is only the beginning of the enterprise."

David Livingstone died in Africa on April 29, 1873. His body was embalmed by his followers, then carried hundreds of miles to Zanzibar. Eventually it arrived in England for entombment in Westminster Abbey with rich praise for Livingstone's courage and determination in the face of extreme difficulties in the country he had learned to love.

MOTHER TERESA

"I Am Not Important"

H ave you ever heard of Agnes Gonxha Bejaxhiu? It's doubtful. Have you ever heard of Mother Teresa? Most likely.

They are the same person, separated only by given name and adopted name and now, citizenship. For Yugoslavian-born Agnes Bejaxhiu, now Mother Teresa, became an Indian citizen in 1948.

1948. An important year for the Irish-trained nun, as that was when she put aside the relative comfort of the Loreto Order to don a white sari with a blue border and a cross on the shoulder. It also was the year she opened her first slum school in Moti Jheel, Calcutta, one of the initial steps in what has become her total dedication to the poorest of the poor.

Remarkably, Mother Teresa doesn't think of herself as remarkable. Yet this petite human dynamo, driven by the word of God, has created a network of homes, shelters, aid stations and people – mostly people – who now give aid to thousands of the wretchedly poor in India and many other nations. And she did it all by faith.

The story of Mother Teresa goes back to Yugoslavia and 1910, where Agnes Gonxha was born into the Bejaxhiu family – Albanians, living then in Skopje. Agnes was one of three children, having a brother and sister, in a deeply religious family. The family encouraged her when she entered the Loreto Abbey in Dublin to prepare to serve as a nun in India, where the Loreto order then was working with the Calcutta Archdiocese.

As Sister Teresa Agnes, she began her novitiate in Darjeeling, India in early 1929, teaching geography in St. Mary's High School in Calcutta. (She later was to become principal of the school.) She took her first vows at Darjeeling in 1931, and her final vows on May 24, 1937. And, as the years passed, she performed as well as was expected of her, though her life then gave no portent of what was to come.

Teresa's life changed on September 10, 1946. On a train to Darjeeling she heard the call of God, telling her that she must work with the poor. She applied to Rome to work outside the cloister in the Calcutta slums and in August, 1948 made the change that altered her life and that of hundreds – actually, thousands – who have since come under her influence.

Many were suspicious of Teresa when she moved into the slum. Some thought she was just seeking publicity, even though she immediately began using a three-months medical course at the American Medical Missionary to give care to the homeless, the ill, the destitute who were in her lowly sphere. Even the church was somewhat concerned about her activities.

But Teresa quickly dispelled doubts. Not only did she work tirelessly herself, but she began to find others who would join her, and so the new Congregation of the Missionaries of Charity was born, with its Mother House a donated building on Lower Circular Road in Calcutta.

For Teresa – now Mother Teresa – total dedication to her service to the poor was matched only by her belief that she was not *working* for lepers or the dying, that her vocation was to belong to Jesus. "Because I belong to Him, the work is a means for me to put my love for Him in action. So it is not an end, it is a means."

Originally, Mother Teresa and her new recruits provided food and medical care for the poor. Then she started a school, next a place where the dying destitute could receive a peaceful end. At each developmental step, Mother Teresa's powerful personality and commitment made converts of even the most skeptic. Though strong in her own Catholic beliefs, she gave comfort to persons of all religions without concern for their own beliefs.

Knowing that God would provide, Mother Teresa simply did what she saw that had to be done. As the Missionaries of Charity order grew, so did its network of homes and shelters, some for the dying, some for lepers, others just to take care of the terminally poor. Gifts of money and donations of property helped the cause, and within a few years Mother Teresa was becoming widely recognized as a person for whom sainthood would not be a compromising mantle.

Mother Teresa has received many honors for her ceaseless efforts with the poor. Among them – above the rest – was the Nobel Prize for Peace, awarded to her in 1979. Characteristically, she used the monetary portion of the award to establish new shelters, buy much needed medical supplies, and generally broaden the work of the Missionaries of Charities. At the time of the award, Mother Teresa said it should not go to her, rather it should go to the poor, who were finally being recognized.

But it was Mother Teresa, confronted as she was by some of the world's worst slums and every form of human misery, who brought aid and hope to the people. Even so, she told a biographer:

"I am not important. Write about the work and the people."

ROY CAMPANELLA

"Reaching Never Hurt a Man"

"Every night when I go to bed, I pray to God and thank him for giving me the ability to play ball."

Those are the words of Roy Campanella, one of the all-time greats of major league baseball, and the first black catcher to play in the big leagues after Jackie Robinson had broken baseball's color barrier.

Campy, as the then Brooklyn Dodger catcher was known, grew up in Philadelphia. A big youngster, he loved playing baseball more than about anything, and had his first try as a professional ball player at age 15 when he began catching in the Negro Pro League. A teammate gave Roy advice that stuck with the teenager:

"Don't aim small. *Reaching* never hurt a man, no matter what color. Remember, success isn't going to chase you. You got to go after it."

Roy played first for the Bacharach Giants, a Philadelphia team, but he quickly came to the attention of the Baltimore Elite Giants of the Negro National League, then the top team.

Roy convinced his parents that he could make a living playing baseball, and they allowed him to leave school the day after his 16th birthday, November 20, 1937. For the next seven years Roy played in the United States during the summer time, and in either Mexico or Puerto Rico in winter. He was playing baseball 52 weeks a year.

Campy was married at 19, and two children were born

of the union, but as the catcher was rarely home, the marriage ended in divorce.

Branch Rickey, owner of the Dodgers, brought Roy into major league baseball. Campy played half a season at St. Paul, an American Association team in the Dodger organization, and Roy was the first black to play in the American Association. However, he was quickly pulled up to the parent club and became a regular behind the plate for the Dodgers.

Campy made his mark quickly on the National League. A fast-throwing, long-ball hitting catcher, he was named the League's Most Valuable Player in 1951, 1953 and 1955 – a period when the Dodgers were winning the World Series regularly.

Roy was recognized off the field, too. In 1953 he received the B'nai B'rith Association plaque for high principle in sports. He also was named player of the year by the New York Sports Writers. Roy had achieved status and good fortune as a ball player, meeting his own highest goal.

Roy invested some of his Dodger earnings in a liquor store in Brooklyn, and during the off season was active in the management of the store. He had worked late at the store the night of January 28, 1958, and was returning home when he hit an icy stretch of road about two miles from home. Roy lost control of the rented car he was driving (his own car was in for repairs) and hit a telephone pole. The car turned over, then landed on its right side. Roy was slammed forward and down onto the floor of the passenger side, his body jackknifed and wedged in under the dash. Roy couldn't move, and knew he was paralyzed when he tried to turn off the motor. His neck was broken, and his spinal cord nearly severed.

Roy was discovered by the town policeman shortly after the accident and medical aid was summoned.

Hospitalized immediately, Roy began a long period of bitterness and despair at his misfortune. He contracted pneumonia in the hospital and nearly died, but his worst problem after the basic injury was his emotional state. Roy refused to see people, and felt sorry for himself.

Eventually a doctor told Roy the fight for his recovery was about 10 percent theirs and 90 percent his. Roy finally began bringing himself back to reality through his faith, particularly through the 23rd Psalm.

Though restricted to a wheelchair, Roy eventually was able to get back and work with the Dodgers as a coach with the young catchers who were taking his place. Though some people tried to suggest that maybe the Lord had turned His back on him, Campy concluded:

"It's good to be alive. Man, it's the mostest thing there is, and anytime you feel different, don't be afraid to go down on your knees and talk things over with the Lord."

For Roy Campanella was one who believed.

ANDREW JACKSON

"Up From the People"

I t was said of Andrew Jackson, seventh President of the
United States, that he was "a lawyer by profession, a
fighter by preference, and a politician through circumstance." Above all, Jackson was one of the most unusual –
and most popular – leaders of his country.

Rough and unconventional, unable to write or speak
"correct" English, lacking social graces, provincial and
harboring a violent temper, Jackson hardly seems the
type of personality that would find himself in the
Presidency. Yet he served two terms, and left office with
as much or more popularity than when he was elected.

Jackson grew up fighting. And hating. The British and
Indians were at the top of his hate list. During the
Revolution, British soldiers had killed his two brothers
and the mother he idolized. Andrew was made a prisoner
of war at age 14, and was brutally slashed by the saber of
an officer whose boots he refused to clean. On the
frontier of Tennessee he learned firsthand of atrocities
attributed to Indian warriors, and at that time there was
no forgiveness in his heart.

The men who had preceded Jackson in the Presidency,
from Washington through Monroe, had all belonged to
the social aristocracy of the young country, and were
gentlemen of wealth, education and refinement. Jackson
was just the opposite. As the first to rise from the
common people to top leadership of the country, he was

the champion of the masses. Yet his intense hatred extended to political and personal enemies, some of whom he dueled as was the honor code of the day.

Why such popularity? No doubt it had to do with battlefield heroics, but it was Jackson's innate leadership ability that elevated him to positions where he attracted attention. Yet, nothing in his birthright would have indicated that he might rise to such a position in history.

Andrew Jackson was born in March, 1767, in the Waxhaw region of the Carolinas. At the age of nine, he was selected from among schoolmates to read aloud the then circulating Declaration of Independence at a country crossroads store, a document he soon took to heart because of personal losses. Orphaned at 14 when the British killed his family, he carried on with his life, including reading enough law to be admitted to the bar before he reached his majority.

At the close of the Revolutionary War, Jackson moved across the Appalachian Mountains to the eastern part of Carolina, where he took part in the establishment of the new State of Tennessee, helping frame its constitution. While residing at Nashville, he was a prosecuting attorney, determined to establish frontier law. Elected as Tennessee's representative to Congress in 1796, he became a senator the following year.

But, it was during the War of 1812 that Jackson rose to national prominence, first as an Indian fighter at the head of the frontier militia, then with bold attacks and defeat of British troops at Pensacola and New Orleans. The latter victory was achieved in ignorance of the fact that a peace treaty already had been signed in Europe. Jackson added to his fame by putting down a Seminole Indian uprising in Florida in 1818, followed by appointment as military governor of the newly acquired territory.

Riding on his popularity, Jackson made his first bid for

the Presidency in 1824. Though he received a plurality of votes, the House of Representatives, to which the decision was referred constitutionally, picked John Quincy Adams, a decision that gnawed at Jackson. Nonetheless, his popularity remained firm, and four years later he was elected President by a large majority of electoral ballots. Political leaders of the day were chagrined: Daniel Webster, among others, predicted the frontiersman would be overthrown.

However, Andrew Jackson's enemies and detractors underestimated his skills just as they had his popularity. He proved to be an able president, and maintained the backing of the people through two terms in office. Of his life, the 19th Century historian Bancroft was to write:

"No man in private life so possessed the hearts of all around him; no public man of the country ever returned to private life with such an abiding mastery over the affections of the people. He was wholly, always, and altogether sincere and true. Up to the last he dared to do anything that was right to do. He united personal courage and moral courage beyond any man of whom history keeps a record."

Andrew Jackson exhibited that courage once again late in his life when he accepted Christ as his savior, for it meant that he had to forgive his enemies. For Jackson this step was a shock. He easily could forgive political foes, but for those who had abused him while he was serving his country in the field, it was a different matter. In the end, Andrew Jackson put aside his hatreds and stood before a congregation and pastor, and, childlike, confessed his faith and was baptized. As his historian had stated, Andrew Jackson, one who believed, "dared to do anything that was right to do."

ERNEST GORDON

"Miracle in a Death Camp"

S cotsman Ernest Gordon, ready to do duty for the
Crown in the early phases of World War II, was
commissioned as an officer in the Second Battalion of
the 93rd Highlanders, a unit soon sent to Malaya, where
British Empire holdings were being threatened by
advancing Japanese land forces.

In the late months of 1939 and early 1940, the British
defenders including the Highlanders, tried to hold
Singapore. But by mid-February they had run out of
ammunition, water and hope, and the colony fell.
Gordon's battalion had been reduced from 1000 men
to 30 survivors.

Gordon escaped from Singapore, crossed Sumatra by
himself to Padang, where he hoped to get aboard a troop
ship that would take him to Ceylon, across the Indian
Ocean. Instead, he ran into a British colonel who was
planning an escape to Ceylon by small boat. Gordon and
several other officers joined forces.

But, their luck ran out 500 miles at sea, when they
were captured by a Japanese tanker, and returned to
Singapore. For the next several years, Ernest Gordon was
a prisoner-of-war.

Very early in his imprisonment, Gordon learned that
the Japanese would not adhere to either the Geneva or
The Hague Conventions concerning treatment of POWs.
Prisoners were shot, bayoneted, drowned, tortured and

starved. Their religion became very important to the men if they were to survive.

The prisoners were moved by train from the Singapore area to a camp at Baipong. Then they were moved on foot to Chungkai camp in the valley of the River Kwai, where they were forced to build a railroad for the Japanese army. They also built the fabled bridge over the Kwai.

Seven days a week the prisoners were marched out of the camp to the place where they were hacking the route for the several-hundred-mile railroad out of the jungle. The men worked naked, except for G-strings, in 120 degree heat. Many died.

Dying was easy. Despair rampant. Gordon noted:

"I mean nothing. Nothing matters; I live only to die."

Prisoners died simply because of the failure of the will to live. Often they were concerned only with themselves. Acts of meanness, suspicion and favoritism permeated their existence. The weak were trampled, the ill ignored, the dead forgotten.

As the months of imprisonment stretched into years, men stole from each other, and continued other acts of faithlessness. Hate of the Japanese became the only motivation for living, but in time, even hate gave way to bleak despair. If men kept faith alive in their hearts, they didn't show it. There was no church, no chaplains, no services.

Gordon contracted diphtheria, beriberi and dysentery. He couldn't walk or work. He was sent to the Death House, "a sordid, snuffing-out place – not-with-a-bang-but-a-whimper – place."

But then a strange change began to come over the camp. Gordon was nursed back to health by two other prisoners – the first act of kindness toward a fellow POW that he had witnessed. And he was not alone. Men were turning away from death to life. They began helping each other in many ways. Generosity became contagious, as did love, self-sacrifice and serving – all human values that had been missing. As Gordon later wrote:

"We began to feel the miracle that God was working in the Death Camp by the River Kwai."

When Gordon had his health back, he was asked by some Australian prisoners to meet with them to discuss Christianity. Gordon, using a New Testament he had secreted, helped the Aussies study Jesus. Before long, men began to smile, even laugh and sing. Others joined the nightly meetings.

Learning of all kinds became important to the POWs. Classes were organized in many subjects as different men showed expertise. The POWs discovered there were many books in the camp, and they wrote others in order to build a library.

With six violins sent in a Care package as the basis, an orchestra was formed in the camp. Some members made their own instruments. Gordon wrote:

"I once thought there were two kinds of food – one for the body, one for the soul. And, of the two, the latter is more satisfying."

It was that food of the soul that kept Ernest Gordon alive to final liberation at the end of the war. For Ernest Gordon was one who believed.

CORRIE TEN BOOM

"All Things are Possible"

W hen Corrie ten Boom was born in Amsterdam,
Holland in 1892, she was described as "a darling,
ugly baby with beautiful eyes." Corrie quickly outgrew
the word "ugly" and became one of the most remarkable
Christians of the 20th Century.

Corrie's parents were a couple who enjoyed life and
loved children, and they welcomed the daughter into
their young family. At the time she was born, Corrie's
father was a jeweler in the Jewish sector of Amsterdam.
Later, when her grandfather died, they moved back to
the family home at Haarlem.

Corrie learned to read when she was five years old,
and particularly enjoyed the stories of Jesus, who was
considered a member of the ten Boom family. She
displayed an affection and concern for her fellow
members of mankind at an early age, praying nightly
for the drunks who slept in the streets, and for the
feeble minded.

The ten Booms were devout Christians, members of
the Dutch Reformed Church. Corrie's father continually
was bringing guests to the house, and intellectual and
theological discussions involved the children as well as
the adults. Corrie read constantly.

When she was 17, doctors thought Corrie had
tuberculosis, and confined her to bed. A misdiagnosis
was corrected when it was discovered she had appen-

dicitis instead. This was a period in her life when Corrie became heavily involved in a study movement for foreign missions. She stretched her personal horizons when she attended missionary camp at Lunteren, where she met people from many other areas. One who influenced her life was Scender Singh, an Indian who first had denied God, but then had a vision of Christ and became a believer. Singh told Corrie:

"That I know Jesus is alive is no miracle – these eyes have seen Him. But you, who have never seen Him, know His presence. Isn't that a miracle of the Holy Spirit?"

Though class distinction was strong in Holland, it was not known in the house of Casper ten Boom. Every human being was someone of value to Corrie's father, a trait he instilled in his daughter. A self-taught Biblical scholar, Casper often said:

"The highest potential of God's love and power is available to us in the trivial things of every day life." He lived as he thought.

After World War I, Casper ten Boom organized a movement to take in orphaned German children, and it wasn't long before the ten Boom house was loaded with extra beds as new members joined the household. At one point they had eight foster teenagers. As Corrie's mother had died, Corrie and her sister were in charge of children. Corrie commented:

"We experienced that with men there are impossible situations and circumstances, but with God all things are possible."

This opening of the ten Boom's hearts and home carried on through World War II, also. Corrie's brother, William, studying in Germany in 1930, noticed considerable anti-Semitism, and accurately predicted that "the severest pogrom in the history of the world would come to Germany." At great danger to themselves, the ten Booms hid persecuted Jews during the war, until their actions were discovered by the Nazis. Corrie, her father, and her sister were imprisoned. As they entered a concentration camp, Casper ten Boom said: "Remember, Corrie, thé best is yet to be." Ten days later he was dead. Corrie's sister also died in prison.

Miss ten Boom spent many months in the concentration camp because of her underground activities, but her faith sustained her. As Corrie would say:

"The ground upon which I build my faith is not in me, but is in the faithfulness of God."

Corrie ten Boom acted on her early missionary training after World War II when she became what she called "a tramp for the Lord," taking the Christian message to thousands of people in 60 countries. On one of her trips she met a Stundist (a member of a group of Christian women in Siberia) who told her she prayed for Corrie daily. The woman had read about Miss ten Boom in a magazine article that was part of the stuffing in a Care package. Corrie ten Boom, one who believed, noted:

"It never ceases to amaze me the way the Lord creates a bond among believers which reaches across continents, beyond race and color."

GEORGE WASHINGTON CARVER

"Show Me What to Do With a Peanut"

T he World Book Encyclopedia has a question mark
behind the listed date of birth of the black American
scientist George Washington Carver, indicating
uncertainty as to his nativity. But, there is no question
mark or uncertainty as to the contribution Carver made
to his people, to education in general, and to the
agriculture of the south. There he stands virtually alone.

Carver was believed to have been born in 1859 on a
farm near Diamond Grove, Missouri, the son of a slave
named Mary and an unknown father. When he was but a
baby, Carver, his mother and a sibling were stolen from
their master, Moses Carver. Moses Carver hired a man to
find "his property" and bring them back, but the searcher
never caught up with the gang who had ridden off with
the trio. But, after six days the man returned to the
Carver farm, bearing a small bundle under his coat. That
bundle was George Washington Carver, more dead than
alive, and too sick for the slave stealers to bother with
him. He had been given to some women in Arkansas,
because "he wasn't worth anything."

As we now know, the baby who had no value survived,
and grew up to a distinguished career in plant research
that revolutionized agriculture in the south. He who was
worth nothing made such a contribution to his people
and to his chosen field that his worth is immeasurable.

It never was easy for Carver to attain the learning for

which he thirsted so strongly, even as a young child. Schools in his area restricted their enrollment to white children, but finally, at age 14, he found a school at Neosho, Missouri that would accept him as a student.

Carver walked to Neosho, and, tired from the journey, rested in front of the residence of Mariah Watkins, midwife and washerwoman, who somehow recognized promise in the young man and took him into her home. Once, trying to thank her, Carver was quoted as saying he was lucky to have picked her yard to rest in. But Mariah retorted: "Luck had nothing to do with it. God has work for you, and he wants me and Andrew to lend a hand."

With sheer determination to learn all he could, Carver applied himself rigorously to his studies. Always curious about plants and rocks, he committed to memory hundreds of species as he completed his pre-college education. Then he enrolled in Simpson College, Indianola, Iowa.

With the help of friends who recognized his genius, and by taking in laundry and working as a janitor, Carver studied first at Simpson and then Iowa State College, from which he was graduated in 1894. He accepted a position as an assistant botanist at Iowa State, taking charge of the institution's greenhouse. There he started a fungus collection that rapidly grew to about 20,000 species. The collection brought him professional fame.

Recognition of the scientist did not go unnoticed by Booker T. Washington, founder of the struggling Tuskegee Institute in Alabama, an institution dedicated to improving the educational opportunities for black citizens. Washington could offer Carver "neither money nor fame" but he did offer a challenge to help in the task of "bringing a people from degradation, poverty, and waste to full manhood." Carver accepted.

If Carver ever regretted the decision to join Washington at Tuskegee, he never let it be known, for it was at the Alabama institute that he unleashed his scholarly attention to agricultural research, determined to find replacement crops for the fickle cotton industry in the South. Carver urged southern farmers to plant peanuts, which they did, only to find there was no market for their crop. Carver went to work in his laboratory, and in the ensuing years helped develop more than 300 commercial products that used the peanut. He had similar success with pecans and sweet potatoes, giving southern farmers options they had not previously had available.

George Washington Carver was a deeply religious man, who thought he was merely acting in response to the direction God had chosen for his life. He received international fame for his work in the laboratory, yet always felt that stimulating the creative initiative of black students was part of his life's mandate. He is known to have turned down an offer of $100,000 to leave Tuskegee to work in Thomas Edison's laboratory, but monetary riches were not his concern.

Carver prayed daily, rising early to communicate with his God at an hour when most people were sleeping. He felt that was when he could hear God best, and learn His plan. When asked the secret of his success, Carver said it was simple, and that it was found in the Bible: "In all thy ways acknowledge Him, and He shall direct thy paths." At a Senate hearing where he had testified about peanuts, Carver was asked how he had learned so much. Carver replied, "From an old book." When asked what book, Carver replied, "The Bible." "Does the Bible tell about peanuts?" a Senator questioned. "No, Senator," the aging scientist replied. "But it tells me about the God who made the peanut. I asked Him to show me what to do with the peanut, and He did."

George Washington Carver died in 1943, the recipient of numerous awards and honors from Presidents, institutions, and private citizens. A national monument was established on the 210-acre Missouri farm that was the site of his birth. On the tombstone of this gentle man, one who believed, were inscribed the words:

"He could have added fortune to fame, but caring for neither, he found happiness and honor in being helpful to the world."

JIM ELLIOT

"From Grace to Grace"

W hen Oregon native Jim Elliot was a student at
Wheaton College in Illinois, he wrote a credo in
his journal:
   "He is no fool who gives what he cannot keep to gain
what he cannot lose."
   Jim Elliot was the son of an evangelistic father and a
chiropractor mother who had moved to Portland in 1922.
Jim, the third of four children, was born in 1927. Father
Elliot daily read Scriptures to the children and the
children heard the call of Jesus at an early age. Jim,
particularly, was an ardent follower as a youth.
Obedience and honesty were stressed in the home, and
when the children were 14, they were told they then were
responsible to the Lord for their actions.
   Jim had a keen mind and wide-ranging interests. He
developed a love for the outdoors through visits to the
Oregon coast and to Mt. Hood, but he also was an avid
reader, built model ships and airplanes, and collected
stamps. Most of all, he developed a religious zeal which
he followed unabashedly.
   In high school, Jim carried a small Bible on top of his
textbooks. He also took an unpopular stand as a
conscientious objector in World War II. Once at a
meeting of the high school public speaking club, he
refused to give a speech for either Presidential candidate
Franklin Roosevelt or Thomas Dewey, saying that "a

follower of Jesus could not participate in war or politics."

Elliot entered Wheaton College in 1945, where he became a top student and a member of the school's wrestling team. At the end of his freshman year, he wrote in his journal:

"How wonderful to know that Christianity is more than a padded pew or a dim cathedral, that it is a real, living daily experience which goes on from grace to grace."

Jim also thought much of his education time could be better spent reading the word of God than in the classroom, commenting: "I do not disparage wisdom – wisdom comes from God, not PhDs."

The young man developed a burning interest in missionary work while in college, especially after a trip to Mexico convinced Jim that God was calling him to Latin America. He majored in Greek at Wheaton, thinking it would help him to an understanding of the basic language of the New Testament, and at some point might help him translate the Bible into some yet unknown native language.

Jim clearly lived by his interpretation of the Bible. No ascetic, he enjoyed to the fullest all that he believed God had given him to enjoy, but felt it wise to keep from his sphere of activity anything which had the power to distract him from pursuit of the will of God. He kept notebooks in which he wrote his thoughts after daily readings of the Scriptures. Letters to family, even birthday greetings and notes to friends, were heavily laced with Biblical references.

From his days in high school, Jim Elliot had judged his own conduct and probably that of others by a list of "don'ts." Late in his senior year at Wheaton he changed, now believing this was contrary to the teachings of the Apostle Paul. Also, he was cutting himself off from some students he wished to know. Though he always had had many friends, he now participated more in college activities and increased his circle of influence.

Elliot was graduated with highest honors from Wheaton in 1949. After a year working and teaching Bible school in Portland, he went to a 10-week missionary training program at the University of Oklahoma. There Jim learned about the Aucas, a tribe of natives in Ecuador that was untouched by civilization. Jim immediately was inspired to go to the Central American country, to live among the Quichas until he could make contact with the Aucas.

Elliot's parents, and others who knew Jim well, thought his ministry should be among the young people at home because of his unusual gift for Bible teaching and preaching, and his ability to relate with the young. But, Jim was determined to go to Ecuador.

It was not until February, 1952, that Elliot finally was able to follow his plans. A friend from Seattle, Peter Fleming, went with him to Ecuador. Eventually they reached Shandia, a jungle settlement, where they lived with the Quichas.

Jim's future wife, Betty, whom he had met in college, also came to Ecuador, and they were married October 8, 1953 in Quito. Their daughter was born February 27, 1955, three years after the day Jim had arrived at Quito.

Jim Elliot at last made contact with the Aucas, and in January, 1956, he and five companions flew into the area where the natives lived. But, in an unexplicable twist of fate, Elliot and the others were killed by the unknown men for whom Jim had prayed for six years. Yet it must be remembered that Jim Elliot, one who believed, wrote:

"He is no fool who gives what he cannot keep to gain what he cannot lose."

In the eyes of God, Jim Elliot had made his trade.

SIR ISAAC NEWTON

"An Ornament of Human Nature"

Sir Isaac Newton, the English philosopher of the 17th century who achieved fame for his studies of mathematics and natural science, also was a devout Christian who contributed many papers through his personal study of theology.

In fact, Newton made the Holy Scriptures as much a study that commanded his attention as any field of science to which he had given thought.

Isaac Newton was born in Woolsthorpe, England in 1642, the year in which Galileo died. Newton's father died several months before he was born, and his mother remarried when the youngster was three years old. Reared primarily by his grandmother, Newton at first was a poor student in school, but when challenged, his natural curiosity for learning and a love of mechanical devices came out. He also enjoyed drawing and writing verse.

Newton attended Grantham School until he matriculated at Trinity College, Cambridge, at the age of 17. Here he was particularly devoted to the study of mathematics, at which he became very knowledgeable. Newton received the degree bachelor of arts in 1664; the following year he left Cambridge temporarily because of the plague.

It was during this absence from Cambridge that Isaac Newton began developing the theory for which he has been best known: the laws of gravitation. Newton began reflecting on the principle one day when he watched an apple fall to earth in his garden.

After Newton returned to Cambridge he worked on his two other remarkable discoveries: fluxions, the nature of lights and colors, and his theory of the universe, detailed in *Philosophia Naturalis Principia Mathematica,* a compilation of his scientific studies published in 1687.

Over the years, Newton became a favorite of the English monarchs, and was knighted in 1705, two years after he was named president of the Royal Society. Accused by a jealous colleague of having developed philosophies that were false and hostile to religion, Newton answered the charge in a manner that was satisfactory to the king. However, his attempt to explain some aspects of Christianity with mathematical demonstration was less well received, and was described by one critic as "being a sort of wandering of a great mind." But he did display a deep reverence for the divine revelation of Christianity in general.

Shortly before he died in 1727, Sir Isaac Newton noted that whatever contributions he had made to the body of knowledge of mankind was through patient and continuous thought rather than to any particular genius with which nature had endowed him. He is reported to have said:

"I know not what I may appear to the world; but to myself I seem to have been only like a boy playing on the sea-shore, and diverting myself in now and then finding a smoother pebble or a prettier shell than ordinary, while the great ocean of truth lay all undiscovered before me."

Sir Isaac was buried in Westminster Abbey, where a monument to his memory contained a Latin inscription that concluded:

"Let mortals congratulate themselves that so great an ornament of human nature has existed." A full-length statue of Newton was erected at Trinity College in 1755.

And, though there may have been controversy concerning Sir Isaac's theology, a biographer, Sir David Brewster, wrote that Newton was "a sincere and humble believer in the leading doctrines of our (Christian) religion, and lived comfortably to its precepts… Cherishing its doctrines and leaning on its promises, he felt it his duty, as it was his delight, to apply to it (Christian truth) that intellectual strength which had successfully surmounted the difficulties of the material universe."

Brewster concluded that Sir Isaac Newton, one who believed, "added to the cloud of witnesses the brightest name of ancient or modern times."

CLARA BARTON

"Think Only of the Need"

When disaster strikes in this country or overseas, often the first group to respond with people and supplies is the Red Cross, an organization that traces its beginning to an informal conference in Geneva in 1863 when several nations sought humane care for battlefield wounded.

The United States was not one of the fourteen countries involved in the founding of the International Red Cross, a circumstance that was later remedied by the tireless efforts of an incredible American humanitarian, Clara Barton.

Miss Barton was a native of Massachusetts, born in the town of Oxford in 1821. A tomboy of sorts, she was a fearless bareback rider on the family horses, and kept up with her active brothers in outdoor sports. But, Clara was painfully shy – shy to the point of becoming ill from the effort to meet strangers or recite in school.

Luckily, Miss Barton found an early release from the phobia, when at the age of 11 she served as nurse for a brother who had been injured in an accident. Clara discovered that in helping others, she helped herself, forgetting her own problems when someone else was in need. It was a discovery that changed her life – and that of thousands of others.

Miss Barton was a schoolteacher for 17 years, where her desire to help her pupils overcame the shyness problem that plagued her. But, it was the outbreak of the Civil War in 1861 that brought on the most remarkable change in Clara Barton, and which led to the founding of the Red Cross in America. Miss Barton was at the train station in Washington, D.C. when many wounded men from the Sixth Massachusetts Militia arrived there in April, 1961. She went to the hospital to help look after these young soldiers and the others who arrived days later as the battles raged on. No one was prepared for such an onslaught of wounded and suffering. But Clara Barton acted: she contacted relatives and friends, asking for donations of food and bandages, and soon had to rent a warehouse for a growing store of supplies. As the war spread, Clara Barton went farther afield, usually caring for sick and wounded right behind the battle lines. Soon she was being called the "Angel of the Battlefield."

Miss Barton had hundreds of narrow escapes from death and wounds herself as she worked tirelessly through the four years of the war, most of it on the front. Even the end of the war did not bring her rest, for President Abraham Lincoln recruited her to try to locate the 80,000 men marked missing on the army records and to communicate with families. It was a task that took another four years.

With her own health at risk, Miss Barton went to Europe in 1869 for a well-earned recuperation. There she was confronted by representatives of the International Red Cross who asked why the United States did not work with the organization. Miss Barton could only reply that the Red Cross was not known in America. When the Franco-Prussian War broke out in 1871, Clara Barton was one of the volunteer nurses again at the front or working with civilians in need, and here she saw the efficiency of the Red Cross. She returned determined to see her country involved with the organization.

It took Clara Barton five years lecturing, leafleting and lobbying to break the Congressional barrier for the establishment of the United States branch of the International Red Cross. That accomplished, Miss Barton found that she was head of a group that had no income and no government participation, only the involvement of sympathetic volunteers. And, as America had no wars, the group actually had no work to be done in this country. It was then that Clara Barton realized that the Red Cross should be involved in other disasters besides war: hurricanes, earthquakes, fires, any calamity that required relief of the suffering. Through her insistence, the constitution of the Red Cross was changed to extend help in these other calamities.

Growth of the organization was slow, and for years Clara Barton *was* the Red Cross in this country. Her Washington home was its headquarters, and she received gifts and dispensed aid without ever being requested to account for the use of money and other gifts, a rare example of public confidence.

Value of the Red Cross became known at the Johnstown Flood, a Galveston hurricane, the Charleston earthquake and hundreds of other disasters. And, at the outbreak of the Spanish-American War, Clara Barton, now 77, was back on the battlefield caring for wounded soldiers. A Red Cross relief ship, the *State of Texas*, was the first American vessel allowed into Santiago after destruction of the Spanish fleet.

When Clara Barton retired in 1904, the Red Cross was reorganized and became recognized as the nation's volunteer relief organization, with the President of the United States as its ex-officio president. What Miss Barton had achieved was widely noted with honors and recognition, earning her the title America's Greatest Heroine.

But this diminutive humanitarian was quick to note that what she had accomplished was done only because she followed a favorite verse of Scripture: "Therefore all things whatsoever ye would that men should do unto you, do ye also unto them." Clara Barton, one who believed, said:

"One must never think of anything except the need and how to meet it. Then God gives the strength, and the thing that seemed impossible is done."

BOBBY RICHARDSON

"A Champion's Role"

From the time he was a very small boy, Bobby Richardson had wanted to be a baseball player. Toward this end, he pestered his Dad to play catch with him every evening, though his father encouraged Bobby's development and was his greatest fan.

Bobby was small, physically, but more than made up for his slight stature with his enthusiasm and his spirit. He was determined to excel. When his Dad wasn't available for "hitting a few," Bobby would throw a baseball against the front steps of his house, catching it as it rebounded.

As he grew older, Bobby began to go to the elementary school playground in his neighborhood, and there he would play baseball as long as anyone would stay with him. This was where he first met a high school student and American Legion ball player named Harry Stokes who was to become Bobby's friend and mentor as Bobby developed his baseball skills.

One of the things about some of the popular athletes in his native Sumter, South Carolina, that impressed young Bobby was the fact that many of them went to church on Sunday carrying a Bible under one arm.

Bobby had his first chance to get into organized baseball when he was ten years old, playing for a Salvation Army team. Since none of the other boys on the team wanted to be bothered with the heavy catcher's

gear, Bobby – the smallest member on the squad –
volunteered for the job behind the plate and played
regularly. His Dad always was in the stands for games,
and frequently Harry Stokes was there, too. Harry
continued to work with Bobby by the hour, perhaps
sensing something unusual in the youngster's desire to
learn the game.

Bobby was very sensitive to mistakes as a team player,
and would brood for long periods if he made a bad play
or didn't hit well. Actually, he was a poor loser, and found
it difficult to recover from a bad game. But, with the
encouragement of Harry and his father, he could be
brought out of these feelings.

Bobby continued to play baseball through high school,
though now he had been moved to the infield where his
quickness and sure hands began to catch the attention of
major league scouts who toured the country seeking new
talent. Yet, even at this time Bobby had the reputation of
being good with the glove, but small at the plate.

At age 14 Bobby Richardson had an experience that
was to change the direction of his personal life. Bobby
had what he considered to be a personal chat with God,
and came to believe that his life's purpose was to please
God. He determined at that point that he would do two
things with his life: he would be a good follower of
Christ, and he would excel at baseball. His conversion
began when he came to believe sincerely that Christ had,
indeed died for *him* – a boy named Bobby Richardson.

Coming off a fine senior year in high school baseball,
Bobby signed a contract with the New York Yankees
organization to play professional ball, a dream he and his
father had had for years. (Bobby's mother was not as
convinced!)

Bobby was given a big send-off by his friends in
Sumter as he left by bus to report to the Yankees Class B

team at Norfolk, Virginia. He was the small-town boy who had made good, and the folks in Sumter were proud to see him go.

But, as often is the case for young men who advance too quickly, Bobby did not play well at Norfolk, particularly since he was joining the team at mid-season and had high expectations for himself. To make matters worse, he had replaced a player who had been a local hero in the Norfolk line-up, and for the first time Bobby had fans jeering and even booing him. After 15 days he was sent to a Yankee Class D team in Olean, New York.

Though disappointed at being dropped down, Bobby found himself at Olean, and began hitting and fielding as he had back home in Sumter. His career finally was on the upswing.

Bobby played the next year at one of the Yankee Class A teams in Binghamton, New York, where he was the starting second baseman. The year had two highlights for him: beating the parent Yankee club in an exhibition game, and meeting fellow ballplayer Johnny Hunton, a devout Christian, from whom Bobby learned that it was possible to be a professional ball player and an uncompromising Christian. Bobby never looked back.

Bobby continued in the minor leagues, with trials at Yankee Stadium, until the 1957 season when he earned his place in the New York pinstripes for good. He went on to a starring role as second baseman for the Yankees, causing one sports writer to say:

"He doesn't smoke, drink, cuss or chew – and he doesn't take a back seat to any second baseman in baseball."

Bobby Richardson, one who believed, achieved his two goals; even as a champion he devoted his life to Christ.

CYRUS HALL McCORMICK

"Put the Hardest Thing First"

I f farmer-inventor Cyrus McCormick had solved a problem that had plagued farmers from the time the first grain was planted, the jeering crowd of onlookers did not believe it when he drove a crude contraption into a Virginia wheat field in July, 1832.

McCormick's machine was the prototype for a grain reaper, a device that finally could free the farmer from the sickle and the scythe, hand tools that made harvesting back-breaking labor. But farmers, in general, are a conservative lot and it was eight years before McCormick sold a single machine. These were eight years of hard toil and much disappointment during which both a farming venture and iron smelting business failed, leaving the inventor bankrupt.

McCormick's break finally came in 1840, a year after he had demonstrated an improved reaper that could cut two acres of wheat in an hour. A farmer who had seen that demonstration bought a reaper, risking all of $50 on the machine. Two years later McCormick sold seven machines, and by 1844 fifty machines. By the time Cyrus McCormick died, in 1884, his Chicago factory was turning out 50,000 reapers a year and the giant industry he had developed led the world in the production of harvesting machinery.

A person of less perseverance might never have seen his invention get to market. But Cyrus McCormick was a person who believed in hard work, just as he believed in God. His plan of work was "one thing at a time and the hardest thing first." Following the line of *most* resistance, McCormick reasoned, made all that came after it easier.

McCormick's tenacity when he considered himself right was demonstrated in a long-running court battle he had with a railroad company that began with an $8.75 excess baggage charge he thought unjust. When finally resolved by the U.S. Supreme Court 20 years later, McCormick was awarded damages and interest amounting to $18,060.79.

When McCormick noticed that many of his orders for reapers in the 1840s were coming from the mid-west, he decided to locate his manufacturing plant in Chicago, then a struggling city of 10,000 persons on the shores of Lake Michigan. He advertised his product in newspapers, and from the beginning his machines were sold with a written guarantee. McCormick often extended credit to the farmers who wanted the reapers, once saying:

"It is better that I should wait for the money than that you should wait for the machine you need."

After the great fire wiped out much of Chicago in 1871, including McCormick's plant, the industrialist considered retiring, even though his factories were turning out 10,000 machines a year. But McCormick's wife urged him to continue in business. With characteristic energy once the decision was reached, he collected all outstanding debts to the company, sold his New York home, and used the available cash to rebuild the plant on even a larger scale.

Just as Cyrus McCormick paid close attention to business detail, so was his devotion to religious principle. He had publicly confessed his faith in Christ at age 25, and in later years when he recognized a need for educated religious leaders he found a theological seminary in Chicago. His contributions to religious work were numerous and varied, and they were carried on for many years after his death by his wife who invested in evangelistic work in more than 25 foreign countries.

A speaker marking the 100th anniversary of Cyrus McCormick's birth noted that McCormick "believed that not only should there be business in our religion and religion in our business, but that religion *is* our business." As McCormick himself once wrote:

"But for the fact that Providence has seemed to assist me in our business, it has at times seemed as if I would almost sink under the weight of responsibility hanging upon me. But I believe the Lord will help me out. How grateful we should be! How humble on account of unworthiness! And yet how rejoicing that, unworthy as we are, we may be saved by faith."

To Cyrus McCormick, one who believed, Jesus Christ was a working partner in a business that could not have grown without His help.

FATHER DAMIEN

"We Lepers..."

The young priest couldn't believe the suffering he found when he arrived at the Hawaiian Island leper colony on Molokai in May, 1873. Of the more than 800 outcasts on the island, most suffered from open sores, twisted, dying limbs, grotesque distorted faces.

Yet Father Damien, a robust, eager native of Belgium, had gone to the island voluntarily, knowing that as he did so he was dedicating his life to these people.

Father Damien, born Joseph de Vuester in Temeloo, Belgium in 1840, was the son of peasants who had a small farm. Devout catholics, the de Vuesters had raised their six children to love God. Though young Joseph went to school to become a businessman, he found his calling as a priest. He was the second de Vuester to take vows, accepting the religious name of Damien.

Father Damien went to the Hawaiian Islands as a missionary in 1864, and for nine years was a parish priest on the island of Hawaii. It was there that he first became aware of the plight of lepers, for he saw families broken apart when a victim of the dread disease would be banished to the leper colony on Molokai.

When the call came for a volunteer to serve the church at the leper colony, Father Damien stepped forward eagerly, having no fear of the disease. But he was warned that he would have to stay on Molokai for life.

Though the priest was used to the casual life style of

the native Hawaiians, nothing had prepared him for the conditions he found on Molokai. The disease victims lived in poorly made huts, surrounded by their own waste and filth, with no clean water or sanitation facilities. Dead were dumped in shallow trenches, often left uncovered. Though the stench in the colony was almost overpowering, Father Damien had hope and knew he would find ways to help the people. He was strong, and ready to do the work he felt he had to do.

Father Damien received no welcome on the island. He belonged to the race the Hawaiian natives believed had brought the disease to their paradise, and they reacted to him much the way they, themselves, had been treated by non-lepers. But his concern for their welfare, and his hard work to improve their living conditions soon had them convinced that this was a man who cared.

Damien first fixed up the church, which long had been neglected. With hours of cleaning and repair, he had it respectable. Someone brought him a gift of flowers, another fruit to eat. In the weeks and months that followed, the priest went daily from hut to hut, washing sores, treating wounds, and even acting as a surgeon with the aid of crude instruments and a medical book. Mainly, though, he gave spiritual relief to victims, and leadership to their efforts to help themselves.

With the guidance and hard work of the strong priest, about 300 huts were rebuilt, all on platforms to keep them dry when the rains came. Gardens were planted between the huts. Father Damien even engineered a new fresh water system from a clear, deep pool high in the hills behind the village.

All the time the priest fought with the Hawaiian government to provide more care for the victims. Lumber was provided for the huts, and pipe for the water system, but no one would set foot on the island to help.

Father Damien conducted weddings, baptisms, and frequent funerals at the colony, and even built the rough coffins himself for the more than 300 victims who died there each year. During his first six years on Molokai he dug the graves and buried nearly 1600 people.

From the beginning, the priest began his weekly church service with the words "we lepers," for he was one of them in spirit if not in fact. In truth, he knew it was a question of time: no cure or treatment was then known for leprosy. Yet he never hesitated to hold a twisted hand, wash a sore-infested body, or lift a victim into a coffin.

Eventually a doctor came to the island to provide medical treatment in the hospital that Father Damien had rebuilt. The physician brought with him new medications that could control leprosy, though there still was no cure.

Father Damien had lived on Molokai 16 years when the disease struck him down in 1889. After his death, stories of his sacrifice went throughout the world, focusing attention on needless suffering by the victims. Agencies were established in India, China and Africa to help lepers, and medical treatment provided relief.

A cross monument erected on Molokai to honor Father Damien, bears the Biblical words, "Greater love hath no man than this, that a man lay down his life for his friends." For though he died a martyr, Father Damien, one who believed, had demonstrated that he and the God he worshiped truly cared.

DANIEL WEBSTER

"Liberty and Union, Now and Forever"

He lived in a time when a man who honed his intellect on the pointed phrases and sharp edges of the Constitution of the United States would rise to power and glory, and thus Daniel Webster – statesman, senator and orator without equal – did.

Yet Daniel Webster, one of the country's best known and most honored political figures of the 19th century, had a bitter disappointment that to him clouded his otherwise distinguished career. He never was given the opportunity to be President of his country.

It is not that he wasn't qualified. Perhaps no man was better qualified, certainly at the time Webster lived. He was elected to the House of Representatives and to the Senate, and twice served as Secretary of State. Yet four times when he sought his party's nomination for the Presidency, it was offered to someone else.

Who was this man whose boldest desire eluded him; whose name today is associated (wrongfully) with the dictionary that he didn't write?

Daniel Webster was a New Englander, born in Salisbury, New Hampshire in January, 1782, just six years after the founding of this nation that he came to prize and defend. Ninth in a family of ten children, Daniel was so frail as a youngster that he was not required to toil on the farm that provided the food and life for the Webster family. Oddly, this man who became known as the greatest orator America ever has produced, was a shy child, afraid to recite in school. But his mind already was absorbing ideas and thoughts with alacrity. Daniel could not remember the time he was unable to read the Bible, a book that he devoured as a child and read thoughtfully each year of his adult life. Once he overcame the shyness that haunted him as a child, he was recognized as a gifted student, entering Dartmouth College at the age of 15. He also was unselfish, for two years later he interrupted his own education to go to work to help support his brother's quest for learning.

Young Daniel studied law in Boston, and was admitted to the bar in 1805 at the age of 23, having become a skilled debater and a person whose physical attributes decried his childhood frailness. Elected to Congress in 1813, he quickly became recognized as the foremost Constitutional lawyer in government service, particularly with respect to the authority of the federal government over the states.

It was on the public stage – the speakers' platform – that Daniel Webster stirred audiences in a way not heard before in this country. Not only was he a willing speaker, but he was ready, his knowledge of history and his preparation masterful. Re-elected to the House and then to the Senate, he constantly was in demand as a speaker.

But these were troubled times for the young republic. Secessionist thoughts fomented in the southern states, bringing forth from Daniel Webster the immortal phrase in 1830, "Liberty and Union, now and forever, one and inseparable." So solid was Webster's belief in the Union of the states that he followed a political course of successive compromises in the years that followed, rather than taking positions that he felt would lead to war. A classic middle course found him in support of the Missouri Compromise in 1850, and excluded once again from nomination for the Presidency.

Though Daniel Webster compromised in his political position, he did not in his religious beliefs. "Religion," he said, "is a necessary and indispensable element in any great human character. There is no living without it. Religion is the tie that connects man with his Creator..."

Webster was equally specific in his personal endorsement of the Christian faith, noting: "I believe Jesus Christ to be the Son of God. The miracles which He wrought establish, in my mind, His personal authority, and render it proper for me to believe whatever He asserts."

Webster died in October, 1852, aged 70, a man who began in poverty but ended in the prosperity of his country's honor. And, if he was disappointed that he had not had a chance to become President, he was not disappointed in his faith. For Daniel Webster, one who believed, once said that the most important thought to enter his mind was, "My individual responsibility to God!"

GLADYS AYLWARD

"Other Work to Do"

When German zeppelins dropped bombs on London during World War I, young Gladys Aylward gathered all the neighborhood children from the streets, sat them around her family organ, and pumped furiously while singing hymns at the top of her voice, drowning out the drone of the strange attackers.

It may have been this direct confrontation with adversity that stiffened the back and resolve of tiny Miss Aylward, for against the greatest of odds she got herself to China in 1930 to serve as a Christian missionary.

It isn't clear when or why Gladys Aylward decided to go to China, or how she determined that she could fulfill a special need when there. It is known that while her friends and classmates were attending parties and the cinema, Miss Aylward often would go to church meetings and Christian lectures though she never pretended to be interested in the intellectual side of theology. Hers was a simple, unswerving belief in God and the Bible.

When an opportunity came for Miss Aylward to enroll in the China Inland Mission School in London, she did so eagerly, resigning her position as a parlor maid. Yet, after a few months, she was asked to leave the school, for her academic progress – especially in the theology courses – was not sufficient to give hope that she could ever learn the difficult Chinese language.

Though Miss Aylward left the school, she did not waver from her goal. Taking a position as housekeeper with retired Chinese missionaries she spent off-duty hours preaching in Hyde Park, where skeptical Londoners sometimes jeered the minute evangelist. However, she was not to be denied her fervor. When she learned that an elderly missionary named Jennie Lawson wanted a younger woman to take over her work in northern China, Gladys Aylward immediately applied for the position. Mrs. Lawson responded that if Gladys could get herself to Tientsin, a guide would bring her to wherever Mrs. Lawson was working. Gladys began applying small amounts of her meager salary toward a ticket on the Trans-Siberian Railroad to take her to her dreamed-of land.

With ninepence cash in her pocket, a two-pounds note sewn in her clothing and a suitcase full of food tins, Miss Aylward left London in October, 1930 for the North Sea Crossing and long train ride across the eastern part of the European continent, even though she had been warned that skirmishes between Russian and Chinese troops would interrupt her journey at the Sino-Siberian border. As predicted, the trip was stopped near the border where fighting was taking place, but Miss Aylward, not to be denied, walked part of the way until she could resume her trip by rail. Even the attempted assault by a Russian police agent in Vladivastok did not turn her back.

Eventually Miss Aylward made her way to Tientsin, where she found a large mission. She also learned that Jennie Lawson was in the territory of Shansi, north of the Yellow River, at the walled city of Tsehchou. She exchanged the last of her money for railroad and bus tickets and a Chinese pass that allowed her to go inland. When she finally got to Tsehchou, a month later, she discovered that Mrs. Lawson still was two days by pack mule away at the mountainous village of Yangcheng.

Upon the recommendation of missionaries at Tsehchou, Miss Aylward exchanged her European-style clothes for the rough blue jacket and trousers worn by nearly everyone in the mountains so as not to call more attention to the fact that she was a foreigner. Miss Aylward learned why when she joined Mrs. Lawson a few days later, for the white were considered "foreign devils" by the simple mountain people, and often were covered with mud and spittle when they went among the people.

Though heart-broken by such a reception at first, Gladys Aylward adjusted to a different culture, even overcoming the severe shock of witnessing the beheading of a bandit in the village square. Gradually she earned the respect of the villagers, particularly after intensive study of Chinese dialects allowed her to communicate.

Jennie Lawson and Gladys Aylward opened an inn in Yangcheng, in order to support their work and to spread the word of the Gospel through the mule drivers and coolies who stopped there. After Mrs. Lawson died of injuries received in an accident, Miss Aylward carried on the work of the Inn Of Eight Happinesses (later the subject of a study of her life in the Ingrid Bergman motion picture *Inn of Sixth Happiness*). She gained great favor as a humanitarian when she was appointed foot inspector by the village Mandarin to carry out the central government's decree that female feet no longer would be bound. The position allowed her to travel among the mountains, stopping at village after village, where she told the story of Christ as well as inspected girl babies to make sure they were freed of the bindings.

Miss Aylward once was called to the village prison, where convicts were rioting and soldiers and police refused to enter. The town governor asked her to stop the riot, since she had been preaching that she "had a living

God who would protect her from harm." Miss Aylward was successful in stopping the riot, and also in bringing genuine reform to the conditions under which the prisoners were kept. Her status in the village now soared, and she was given the nickname Ai-weh-deh, virtuous one, by which she was known the rest of her China stay.

Miss Aylward became a naturalized citizen of China in 1936, feeling it would eliminate one of the separations between her and the people she had come to love. It also gave her additional determination to stay with her village after the Japanese invaded Shansi in 1938, causing destruction to the land and homes of people who had never even seen an airplane, let alone one that rained death from the sky.

At first attempting to remain neutral in the war, Miss Aylward eventually decided to aid the Chinese by reporting Japanese troop movements and strengths that she noticed in her travels among the villages. These activities also came after a savage beating she received from Japanese soldiers who had assaulted many women in the Tsehchou mission once while Miss Aylward was visiting there. In the end, her information gathering led to a price on her head by the invaders, forcing her to seek safety south of the Yellow River.

Leading a band of nearly 100 children, Gladys Aylward walked hundreds of miles through the mountains, and crossed the Yellow River, to get to the safety of a mission founded by Madame Chiang-kai-Chek. Miss Aylward completed the journey and delivered the children, though she was suffering from pneumonia, malnutrition, typhus and relapsing fever. When asked later why the seriously ill Miss Aylward did not die, the physician who attended her said: "I can only presume that God has other work for her to do."

And so He did. Miss Aylward not only survived, but

after a ten-year reprieve in Britain, where she preached and lectured on her experiences, she returned to a China now taken over by the forces of Communism. Miss Aylward founded an orphanage in Hong Kong, then moved on to Formosa, where she once again received children wanted by no others.

Gladys Aylward, the self-taught, determined little woman who helped so many to discover the gift of Christ, died on January 2, 1970 in Formosa, the day before film star Ingrid Bergman arrived to visit the woman she had come to admire when she played Miss Aylward's life story. Miss Aylward's biographer, Alan Burgess, summed up her ministry best in his book THE SMALL WOMAN when he said:

"Her kind of Christianity outshone the goodness of popes and bishops and all established churches. And above all she lifted our hearts because of her innocence, her courage, and her passionate belief that through God you can move those mountains which block out a view of the sun."

ERIC LIDDELL

"I'll Not Run on Sunday"

H e was nicknamed the Flying Scotsman, and with good reason. For when Eric Liddell took to the track in the early 1920s, arms flailing, head held high, he generally flew past all opponents in the dash for the tape.

Liddell ran the 100-yard-dash and the 220-yard-dash at Edinburgh University, and had lost only one race in Scotland as he and the world prepared for the coming 1924 Olympics in Paris. But Liddell, a quiet man with strong principles, announced that he would not compete in the 100-meter dash in Paris when he learned a few months before the Olympic games that preliminary heats of the race were to be held on Sunday.

Liddell's fellow Scots were shocked at his decision, as was the entire United Kingdom, though some athletes admired his courage. After all, Liddell was one of the fastest runners in the world, and his entry in the 100-meter dash virtually guaranteed the U.K. a gold medal.

"No," said Liddell, firmly. "I am not running on a Sunday."

Though stung by charges of being a traitor to his country, Liddell did not waver from his decision. For Liddell was a man of simple beliefs, deeply rooted in Scripture. For the Lord, and for him, Sunday was a day of rest but not of play. And running, even in the Olympic Games, was play to a man of Eric Liddell's character.

Instead of the 100-meter dash, Liddell entered the

200-meter dash (where he placed third in the finals), and the 400-meter run, one of the most difficult races in all track competition. Against the finest quarter-milers in the world, Eric Liddell ran the race of his life, not only winning the gold medal for Great Britain, but setting a new world record at the same time.

While his native countrymen celebrated his astounding victory in raucous style, Eric Liddell quietly prayed, giving thanks where he felt it was deserved. He returned home a national hero, sought after for public appearances and speeches and now admired for his noted stand.

Liddell received a standing ovation when he was recognized to receive his bachelor of science degree at Edinburgh University a week after his Paris triumph. And, while at the peak of public adulation, Eric Liddell enrolled in Scottish Congregational College to receive the theological training he desired to return to China as a Christian missionary.

Yes, it was to be a *return* to China, for that is where Eric Liddell and his older brother Robert both were born, and where Eric had lived until his father, the Rev. James Liddell, returned to Scotland for the education of his sons.

Eric was a good but not outstanding student at Eltham College, a preparatory school, where he and his brother Rob rewrote the track record book, and played rugby football and cricket. Sports came easy to Eric: later he occasionally would say he sometimes wished he had chosen the relatively easy life of a professional athlete. Usually it was said with his noted grin, and a twinkle in his clear, blue eyes.

It was while he was at Eltham that Eric Liddell became a communicant of his church. Yet his faith, while firm, remained unspoken until 1923 when he made his first public confirmation at a Christian Evangelistic meeting to which he had been invited to speak by Scottish evangelist D.P. Thompson. Already Scotland's best known athlete, Liddell's reputation had come on the track and rugby field, and this confession brought him new attention, though certainly not the shower that occurred when he decided not to race in Paris.

Liddell's faith was simple, personal. As biographer Sally Magnusson says in THE FLYING SCOTSMAN, "His faith was deep rooted in the evangelical fundamentalist tradition, which accepts the Bible not just as a collection of wise maxims and cautionary tales but as the embodiment of the truth about mankind, about man's destiny and his relationship with God."

Yet Eric Liddell chose not to try to impose his beliefs on others, but instead lived by what he saw to be Christian principles. Modest, unassuming, he selected the obscurity of missionary work in China to the high visibility of professional athletics, though his fans never forgot his exploits on the cinder track.

In 1925 Liddell went to Tientsin, China, the place of his birth, as a teacher in Tientsin Anglo-Chinese College, operated by the London Missionary Society. He returned to a China in the turmoil of civil war, one soon to be invaded by Japanese imperialists. It was there that he met – and later married – Florence McKenzie, daughter of Canadian missionaries. Florence returned to Canada for four years of nurse's training before they wed, and Eric, too, finished his theological training, being ordained in the Scottish Congregational Church in June, 1932.

Eric and Florence frequently were separated after their marriage, even after two daughters were born in quick succession. Eventually, as the war in China spread and the world moved closer to global conflict, their time together was even less, for Eric now went to Siaoching to a field post. There Chinese Nationalists were fighting Chinese Communists, and both were fighting the Japanese.

Eric took no side in the war, seeing "all men as children of God whom He cared for." All were men Christ had died for, thought Eric Liddell.

Eric remained in war-ravaged China in 1941 when he sent Florence and his daughters home. Neither he nor Florence could imagine that this would be the last time he would see his family, and that he would never meet the daughter Florence was carrying as she sailed from their beloved China.

Though the work of the mission was reduced through the early years of the 1940s, Eric Liddell's strength and personality – and faith – made him a natural leader among his fellow anglos in China, and with the people he served. When 1800 British subjects and Americans were interned by the Japanese in late March, 1943, Eric quickly became a subject of inspiration to his fellow internees through his actions and his straight-forward, simple declarations of faith. He *lived* his Christianity in the camp.

Eric Liddell died in that prison camp, just as he had lived, helping his fellow men. A brain tumor claimed his life in February, 1945. After his death, another internee said of Liddell:

"Of all the men I have known, Eric Liddell was the one in whose character and love the spirit of Jesus Christ was pre-eminently manifested."

It had been more than two decades since Eric Liddell had won the hearts of his countrymen on the oval track and their respect with his witness to God. Yet when news of his death reached the outside world, Liddell was eulogized on four continents by those who had not forgotten the Flying Scotsman, one who believed.

BROTHER ANDREW

"Make Seeing Eyes Blind"

T o say that the Dutch missionary who became known
to the world as Brother Andrew always had been an
unswerving believer would be stretching the truth that
became the foundation of his work.

Not, though, for lack of example. Andrew was reared
in the polderland village of Witte, Holland, the son of a
blacksmith father and a deeply-religious but semi-invalid
mother. Though the family was poor, no visitor ever was
turned away from the table.

One Christian neighbor family, the Whetstras, knew
that war with Germany was inevitable, and asked young
Andrew to pray for his homeland. In return, Andrew and
his friends played pranks on the Whetstras, thinking
them to be foolish.

After Holland was occupied by the German forces, 12-
year-old Andrew traded vegetables for fireworks which
he used to harass the invaders. He also put sugar in the
enemy commandant's gas tank. Long before the
occupation was over, food ran out in the village and the
Dutch ate tulip bulbs to survive. Able-bodied men and
boys were conscripted into German work forces; Andrew
joined others who constantly had to hide from
the Germans.

In 1946, after World War II, Andrew, 17, joined the
Dutch army to go to the Dutch East Indies, where there
was rebellion after liberation from the Japanese. Andrew

trained as a commando, and once commented:

"Part of the education of a commando was the development of self-confidence. But here I needed no schooling. From childhood I had had a completely unfounded confidence in my ability to do anything I set out to do."

Destruction of an Indonesian village by Dutch troops drove Andrew to extreme behavior. He hated himself for what he and his countrymen had done, and began wearing a yellow straw hat into combat as if to dare the enemy to kill him. Eventually he was seriously wounded in the foot – an injury that doctors told him would prevent him from ever walking normally again.

While in the hospital, Andrew began reading the Bible that his mother had placed among his belongings when he left for overseas duty. Though he did not understand all he read, the words seeped into his consciousness. A major change came for the young soldier after he was sent home. At a revival meeting which he and other hospitalized veterans attended, the words of a hymn – "Let My People Go" – began to make an impression on Andrew. Now when he turned to his Bible, the words had meaning for him.

Andrew began attending church regularly and even made notes from the Scriptures and sermons which he checked against his own Bible. Finally, alone, in the dead of winter in 1950, he gave himself over to Christ with the simple prayer: "Lord, if You will show me the way, I will follow You."

Shortly after proclaiming his faith, Andrew felt a wrenching in his badly-crippled leg. Suddenly he could walk again, without pain. His wound was healed.

Determined to become a missionary, Andrew gained entrance to the World Evangelization Crusade training school for missionaries in Glasgow, Scotland. Near the end of his training he learned of a youth festival in Warsaw. Andrew made his first trip behind the Iron Curtain in July, 1955 to attend the festival, taking with him copies of a small tract THE WAY OF SALVATION which he passed out to members of churches and even to Polish soldiers. That visit was the beginning of a crusade for Andrew, for he soon realized that Bibles were a rare item beyond the frontiers of the free world, and he was determined to get them to believers in the Communist realm.

Upon his first opportunity, Andrew loaded Bibles into the car given him by his former neighbors, the Whetstras – who supported his missionary zeal – and drove toward Yugoslavia. As he approached the border with boxes and suitcases full of contraband literature, he gave the standard prayer that he came to use many more times as God's smuggler:

"Lord, in my luggage I have Scriptures that I want to take to Your children across the border. When You were on earth, You made blind eyes see. Now, I pray, make seeing eyes blind. Do not let the guards see those things You do not want them to see."

At this border crossing, and many more to follow, Brother Andrew passed unchecked. Often he was allowed through gates when other visitors to Communist lands were subjected to searches of cars and luggage.

Through this personal mission, Brother Andrew took the word of God to hundreds of Christians behind the Iron Curtain, often at great personal risk of arrest and sometimes in defiance of authorities who had denied him visas. But Brother Andrew, one who believed, was confident that his mission was God's work, and that He would stay the hand of the oppressor for one doing this duty.

Credits

EDDIE RICKENBACKER: Adapted from *Rickenbacker*, by Edward V. Rickenbacker, reprinted by permission of the publisher, Prentice-Hall, Inc., Englewood Cliffs, N.J., ©1967.

ETHEL WATERS: Adapted from *I Touched the Sparrow*, by Twila Knaack, WORD, Incorporated, Waco, Texas, ©1978.

JESSE OWENS: Adapted from *Jesse*, by Jesse Owens with Paul Newmark, Logos International, Plainfield, N.J., ©1978.

JONI EARECKSON: Taken from *Joni* by Joni Eareckson and Joe Musser. Copyright ©1976 by Joni Eareckson and Joe Musser. Used by permission of Zondervan Publishing House.

GEOFFREY STUDDERT KENNEDY: Adapted from *Woodbine Willie: A Study of Goeffrey Studdert Kennedy*, by William Purcell, A. R. Mowbray & Co., LTD, Oxford, England.

SAMUEL F. B. MORSE: From *More Sources of Power in Famous Lives*, by Walter Erdman. Copyright renewal ©1964 by Walter Erdman. Adapted and reprinted by permission of the publisher, Abingdon Press.

BABE DIDRICKSON ZAHARIAS: Used by permission of A. S. Barnes & Co., San Diego, CA, *This Life I've Led*, by Babe Didrickson Zaharias, 1955.

TOYOHIKO KAGAWA, Adapted from *Saint in the Slums: The Story of Kagawa of Japan*, by Cyril Davey, Lutterworth Press, London, ©1968.

PETER MARSHALL: Adapted from *A Man Called Peter*, by Catherine Marshall, Fleming H. Revell Company, Old Tappen, N.J., 1951.

MOTHER TERESA: Adapted selections from *Mother Teresa: Her People and Her Work*, by Desmond Doig. Copyright ©1976 by Nachiketa Publications. Reprinted by permission of Harper & Row, Publishers, Inc.

ROY CAMPANELLA: Adapted from *It's Good to be Alive*, by Roy Campanella, Little, Brown and Company, Publishers, Boston, MA, 1959.

ANDREW JACKSON: From *More Sources of Power in Famous Lives*, by Walter Erdman. Copyright renewal ©1964 by Walter Erdman. Adapted and reprinted by permission of the publisher, Abingdon Press.

ERNEST GORDON: Adapted selections from *Through the Valley of the Kwai*, by Ernest Gordon. Copyright ©1962 by Ernest Gordon. Reprinted by permission of Harper and Row, Publishers, Inc.

CORRIE TEN BOOM: Adapted from *In My Father's House*, by Corrie ten Boom, Fleming H. Revell Company, Old Tappen, N.J.

JIM ELLIOT: Adapted selections from *Shadow of the Almighty*, by Elizabeth Elliot. Copyright ©1958 by Elizabeth Elliot. Reprinted by permission of Harper & Row, Publishers, Inc.

CLARA BARTON: From *More Sources of Power in Famous Lives*, by Walter Erdman. Copyright renewal ©1964 by Walter Erdman. Adapted and reprinted by permission of the publisher, Abingdon Press.

BOBBY RICHARDSON: Adapted from *The Bobby Richardson Story*, by Bobby Richardson, Pyramid Books. Used by permission of the author.

CYRUS H. McCORMICK: From *More Sources of Power in Famous Lives*, by Walter Erdman. Copyright renewal ©1964 by Walter Erdman. Adapted and reprinted by permission of the publisher, Abingdon Press.

FATHER DAMIEN: Adapted from *Island of No Return*, by Goeffrey Hanks, The Religious Education Press, Exeter, England.

DANIEL WEBSTER: From *More Sources of Power in Famous Lives*, by Walter Erdman. Copyright renewal ©1964 by Walter Erdman. Adapted and reprinted by permission of the publisher, Abingdon Press.

GLADYS ALWARD: Adapted from *The Small Woman*, by Alan Burgess, Evan Brothers LTD, London. Used with permission of Unwin Hyman LTD.

ERIC LIDDELL: Adapted from *The Flying Scotsman*, by Sally Magnusson, Quartet Books, London, 1981.

BROTHER ANDREW: Adapted from *God's Smuggler,* by Brother Andrew with John and Elizabeth Sherrill; Chosen Books Inc., Chappaqua, N.Y., 10514.

Dr. Robert B. Pamplin, Jr.

Businessman, farmer, author, minister Dr. Robert B. Pamplin, Jr. is president of the R. B. Pamplin Corporation, a family-owned company engaged in concrete, sand and gravel mining, asphalt paving, and textile manufacturing. He is also a farmer, French restaurant owner, author of numerous books, and pastor of Christ Community Church.

A graduate of Lewis and Clark College and the University of Portland, Dr. Pamplin holds bachelors and masters degrees in business administration, accounting, economics and education. He has also earned a masters and doctors degree from the Western Conservative Baptist Seminary.

Dr. Pamplin has served on presidential and state commissions, been active on college boards, and has been awarded several honorary degrees.

Thomas K. Worcester

Thomas K. Worcester is a free-lance writer who has authored or co-authored several books, and has contributed to many national and regional magazines. He also has written scripts for radio, film, and slide productions.

A graduate of the University of Colorado with degrees in journalism and educational administration, Worcester is staff writer for Christ Community Church. His professional associations include the Authors Guild, National Writers Club, Western Writers of America, and Northwest Association of Book Publishers.